The Sin of Apathy

Ralph Kerr, Ed.D

Deb
Blessings on your
in your important
work with children
Ralph Kerr

xulon PRESS

The Sin of Apathy
by Ralph Kerr, Ed.D

Printed in the United States of America

ISBN 978-1-60791-132-6

www.xulonpress.com

TABLE OF CONTENTS

Contents

Dedication

This book is dedicated to four important people who have played a vital role in the formation and ongoing work of the Teaching and Learning Institute (TLI Inc.) and particularly the writing of this book.

To my wife Marilyn - Her love, as well as her encouragement, advice, counsel and editorial assistance has provided the motivation to dream another big dream and continue to pursue it to completion.

To my son Gordon, a public school administrator, for his work in the area of future teacher preparation and his ongoing challenge to teachers to be champions of high ethical and moral standards in the classrooms of our public schools.

To my daughter Kim and my son-in-law Terry Pegula for their interest and support in helping to find a way to get more people of faith involved in public education.

Introduction

Public Education in the United States is a $500 billion enterprise. The U.S. Constitution states that children in the United States are entitled to a free public education. From a humble beginning which primarily involved a one room school and one teacher, public education has grown into big business.

Public education is primarily taxpayer funded. In many states voters have the final say in approving or not approving the school expenditures each year. School board members are generally elected to serve their communities and oversee these expenditures. Unfortunately in recent years less than ten (10%) of the people eligible to vote for school board candidates and the budget have taken the time to do so. In nearly 50% of the school districts in which voters have an opportunity to vote for school board candidates there really is no choice. The same number of candidates run for election as there are vacancies. As a result there are no choices for the voters. The control of the expenditures made in public schools has often fallen to the will of teachers unions and other self-serving people. This unfortunate situation has been greatly assisted by the lack of involvement of average people like you and me.

We are indeed guilty of ***The Sin of Apathy.***

The author of this book, a 30 year public school educator, exposes the enemies of public education and thus the injustices that are being done to our children. The public school enterprise established for the good of the children and ultimately for the good of our country and the values it was established upon, has gone amuck in some places. Fortunately it remains strong and vibrant in many other places.

CHAPTER ONE

Public Schools Are In Trouble

"The Board of Education has abdicated its oversight role and essentially failed to monitor the District's financial operation."

"Nearly a quarter (25%) of the school boards in the state are considered highly dysfunctional and ineffective."

"The National Education Association (Teachers Union) recently passed a resolution to endorse, support and promote homosexual and other forms of marriage in their local school districts."

"Nearly one quarter (25%) of the school boards in the state fail to act with a high degree of civility, mutual trust and respect."

"It is hard to ignore the fact that government schools are destroying our children intellectually, morally and spiritually."

The 12th annual edition of Education Week's Quality Counts shows an average grade for Quality Counts 2008 is a "C." States were awarded overall letter grades based on their ratings across six areas of performance and policy:

1) chance for success
2) K – 12 achievement
3) standards, assessments, and accountability

4) transitions and alignment
5) the teaching profession
6) school finance

Three states lead the pack with B's; Maryland, Massachusetts and New York. At the other end, five states plus the District of Columbia were awarded grades of "D+." The five states were Idaho, Mississippi, Nebraska, Nevada, and Oregon.

The same report indicates the Graduation Rate nation-wide is 69.9%. The State of Utah leads the way with an 83.8% graduation rate while South Carolina is lowest with only a 53.8% rate.

These pathetic educational results were achieved with an average per pupil expenditure of $9,138 nationally in 2006. Below are comparative per pupil expenditures from some representative states.

Per Pupil Expenditures By State

New York	$14,884
New Jersey	14,630
District of Columbia	13,446
Arizona	6,472
Idaho	6,440
Utah	5,437

Remember which State had the highest graduation rate, Utah.

Growing anxiety about the public schools

The earlier quotes are representative of the basis for a growing anxiety about the public school system across the United States of America. Today nearly 56 million children attend local K – 12 public schools. In 2006, 41% of these students were minorities. 10.9 million of these children speak a language other than English at home.

Our organization, the Teaching and Learning Institute (TLI Inc.) was created by public school administrators who collectively have nearly 50 years experience in the public school systems of New York State. During our careers we have served the children of the state in school districts ranging from small to large in rural, suburban and small city locations.

During our careers we have seen drastic changes in public education. Some changes have been less than desirable, other changes have certainly been for the good of all involved. Here are some examples of some of the changes we have seen.

We have seen state mandates and expectations for students increase dramatically and fortunately have seen students respond positively.

We have seen the costs of education skyrocket.

We have seen communities demand more and more of school districts and their personnel.

We have also seen less and less involvement and responsibility taken by parents.

We have seen moral and ethical standards decline.

We have seen more and more school boards lose sight of the reason they were created.

We have seen more and more school board members struggle to take over responsibilities which are not theirs to take.

As a direct result of some of these changes some parents, like a representative group within the Southern Baptist Church, have called on their denomination to establish an exit strategy that would remove all children of Southern Baptists from the public school system. Research shows that if all "Christian" students were withdrawn from the public schools, 90% or over 50 million children currently in the system would still remain. Don't we have a responsibility for the 50 million children who would remain? If so, what is that responsibility and what specifically can one individual do to take up that responsibility?

Those of us at the Teaching and Learning Institute believe the best way to become part of the decision making process, and thus affect positive change in our local schools is to serve on the Board of Education.

The public school system in the U.S. is not the sole organization that appears to be in serious trouble and needs help. Look at the current conditions in our world both at home and around the world. Read carefully these recent headlines from abroad.

Israeli strike religious complex; rockets fall on Haifa

Muslims around the world protest Israeli actions

Hezbollah drawing strength from Syria and Iran

Protesters take over Mexican town

China storm death toll nears 500

Dutch commandos kill 18 Afghan militants

Somali militant urges holy war on Ethiopia

International financial markets indicate a world-wide recession

Here are headlines from within the United States.

New wildfires out West

Political debate has reached an all-time low.

Severe weather takes its toll in the Midwest and Southern states.

Dow Jones average looses 700 points today.

And headlines in New York State?

New York Governor resigns in disgrace after being accused of having sex with a high priced prostitute.

New Governor admits sexual relations with a coworker during early years of marriage.

New York State Comptroller resigns in disgrace;

Independent Authority official retires with $233,000 golden parachute.

*Former school superintendent and business official
placed in jail for misuse of taxpayer dollars.*

Unfortunately new disturbing scenarios could be added
to this list on a daily basis by simply reading any local newspaper, listening to the radio or watching television news.

No book or volume of books can speak to all the issues
or concerns mentioned in this list.

The book you are reading has a very specific intention.
It is to address the multitude of issues currently being faced
by the public schools of our nation. The book begins with a
listing of serious concerns the public in general need to be
much more aware of. These serious concerns are raised in
the context of descriptors referred to as "Enemies of Public
Education." Next it offers helpful and practical solutions
for parents, students, educators and also government and
community leaders who are interested in making an impact
on their local public schools. It will specifically outline
the critically important role of the local school board with
its involvement in policy setting, personnel appointments,
particularly the hiring of the superintendent of schools and
establishment of the curriculum to be taught. The book will
also champion the essentiality for citizen involvement at this
level, particularly by people who are committed to family
values based on a traditional Judeo-Christian belief system.

Dr. Rod Paige, former US Secretary of Education in
the George W. Bush Administration states in his book The
War Against Hope "...school board elections in many ways
determine our future. We need organizations to help train
and arm candidates. Such citizen oriented, reform minded
organizations must identify and recruit potential candidates,
and then provide them with information ranging from how
to be a candidate and meet financial and political deadlines
to how to get involved about curriculum and contracts at the
local level."

"Declining involvement in our public schools is alarming"

A former president of the New York State School Boards Association said, "Declining involvement in our public schools is alarming. It is apparent that we need to do a better job educating our residents about the importance of the public school."

Despite these urgent calls for involvement in local public schools, particularly in the election process for school board members, recent statistics nationally reveal that these calls are mostly going unheeded. For example in San Joaquin County, California school board trustees control hundreds of millions of dollars, thousands of employees and educate more than 130,000 students. In the 2006 school year, 37 total people ran for 37 vacancies on local boards. There was not a race for a single position.

In Saco, Maine where the public overwhelming voted to increase the size of the local school board as a result of increased population not enough candidates came forward to provide a legal quorum of the board.

In Washington, D.C., our nation's capital, candidates for two out of three seats (including the school board president's) ran unopposed. The D.C. school board sets policy for a district of 67,500 students, oversees a budget of $938 million and manages a capital building program of more than $2 billion.

In New York State over the last four years nearly 50% of the school districts had the same number of candidates for the local school board election as there were vacancies. In some counties this increased to over 62%. In the 2008 school board elections there were more write-in candidates than ever before. This means there were not enough candidates on the ballot to fill the existing vacancies. In at least one district, even with write-in candidates, there still remained a vacancy on the Board. Some write-ins were elected with as few as 30 total votes. This is very troubling. It means voters had no opportunity to learn the positions, beliefs and values of the candidates in advance of them being elected.

Statewide less than 10% of the eligible voters even took the time to vote for either school board candidates or the school budget. This despite the fact that school budgets in New York State totaled more than $5 billion in 2008. In addition the State of New York distributed $19.7 billion in aid to schools in the 2007-08 budget, $21.5 billion in 2008-09 and are scheduled to distribute $23.3 billion to schools in 2009-10.

Noted writer George F. Will in a column appearing in Newsweek on October 6, 2008 with regard to absent ballots stated, "A word describes most of the people who will vote only if a ballot is shoved through their mail slot; 'slothful.' What kind of people will not bestir themselves to exercise their franchise if doing so requires them to get off their couches and visit neighborhood polling places? The coming of the public into public places for the peaceful allocation of public power should be an exhilarating episode in our civic liturgy."

Perhaps my choice of a title for this book, "The Sin of Apathy" is really on the mark after all.

In some districts in New York State where the school budgets were defeated the margin of defeat was 14, 32 and 39 votes. In talking with many people about this phenomenon it appears voter apathy stems from a variety of reasons, many centered in frustration. They include:

"My vote doesn't really matter. The 'school people' do whatever they want to do."

"The teacher's unions can determine the outcome of the elections and the budget vote by simply getting their members and family members to vote."

"School finance is so complicated no one can understand it anyway."

"The current members of the school board manipulate the election process so that the people they want on the board get elected."

"I received a good education when I was in school and my children seem to be doing all right so why should I take the time to vote."

"Schools are just like other forms of government. The 'little guy' like me can't really make any difference in the way things are done."

Comments like these are really unfortunate. Some of them are simply not true while others unfortunately really describe current conditions. Some statements are made out of ignorance or at least a total lack of understanding. Let's look at some examples that support the truth of some of the statements.

1) <u>The influence of teacher unions.</u> Just last year, for example, the Cincinnati Inquirer reported that Cincinnati school board member Rick Williams looked like an early shoo-in for reelection until a labor backed slate of challengers bolstered by donations that included $10,000 from the Cincinnati Federation of Teachers, took advantage of voter discontent with the city schools and ultimately trounced the incumbent.

Some studies have concluded that if a candidate has the support of the teachers union, there is a 96% chance that candidate will be elected to the board.

2) <u>Inability to make a real difference</u>. Subsequent to the school budget vote in May 2008 a writer to the Buffalo News stated "Voters simply don't have that much to say over spending even though they can vote on the school budget. If the budget is defeated and a contingent budget is put in place most of the programs still continue. Contingency rules do not apply to most day-to-day operations and expenditures. The district would not be able to spend money on new equipment, optional maintenance, or allow community access to the school buildings without charge. Other than these things nothing else changes."

One of the major goals of this book is to give readers an opportunity to learn where truth really lays on these issues. Another goal is to provide readers with a level of understanding regarding the entire educational enterprise. Achievement of these goals will hopefully result in many more people becoming involved in voting not only for school board candidates but also voting for or against their local school district budget.

The 730 school districts in New York State enroll approximately 2.7 million students, employ 470,000 people and have nearly 4000 school board members.

Along with the apathy related to the public not voting for school board candidates and on the school budget another "hot topic" in schools is parental involvement. Perhaps it would be more accurate to say the lack of parental involvement. Many parents say they want to be more involved. Most teachers and administrators decry the lack of parental involvement. So what accounts for this seeming disconnect?

Teachers and administrators claim when they ask for more involvement parents tell them they want to be involved but they simply don't have the time. When parents are asked about lack of involvement they often claim that teachers and administrators tend to make them feel "unwelcome" or even like "intruders" when they offer to be involved. It seems there is a significant need to build a bridge across this chasm.

In Pennsylvania there are 501 school districts, and according to State statistics from 2006, 1.8 million students, 149,260 employees, including 123,374 teachers and nearly 4509 school board members.

Nationwide there are approximately 13,500 school districts, 97,382 public schools, 56 million children enrolled, 7.1 million teachers in these schools, and nearly 95,000 school board members.

Public schools are big business!

Obviously public schools are big business, not only because of the number of districts, the number of students, employees and school board members but also because nearly $500 billion is spent annually on K – 12 public education.

Schools in America – Historically

Governments and public education in the United States actually began in 1647 in New England. At that time towns with more than 50 households were enabled to hire a teacher for writing and reading. Towns of more than one hundred households were required to establish a grammar school to prepare students to attend university. In the early 1900s central boards began to take responsibility for overall policy and a professional superintendent, who could double as the principal, became responsible for the day-to-day opera-tion. As recently as 1933 there were approximately 127,000 school districts across the nation. By the mid-20th century 84,000 school districts existed with at least five Board of Education members per district.

Schools in America – Presently

Today there are 13,500 school districts. The sizes of school districts vary tremendously nationwide. Twenty-one percent of the school districts have more than 2500 students. These districts represent 80% of the total students enrolled in public schools. Seventy-nine percent of the school districts have fewer than 2499 students. This represents 20% of the total students enrolled. The U.S. Census Bureau reports that in the 2004-05 school fiscal year K-12 education had total revenue of $488 billion. $138.6 billion or 28 percent of the revenue was from the local property tax. Yes, K-12 education is a very big and very expensive business. The National School Board Association claims there are 95,000 Board of Education members in the country. School boards in most districts have 5, 7 or 9 elected members. What is the school board? The School Board is a corporate body that oversees and manages the public school districts affairs, personnel, and properties. In most cases its members are elected by the residents of the school district that the board oversees.

So what are the responsibilities of the school board and its members? The primary responsibility of the school board is to set the policy for the district. Policies are the means by which a school board leads and governs its school district. Policies form the bylaws and rules for the governance of the district and serves as standards to which the Board, administration, teachers, support staff and students are held accountable. The board's policies insure that the school district performs its established mission and operates in an effective, uniform manner. A policy is a statement that establishes standards and/or objectives to be attained by the district. A school board policy should clearly state the board's view of what it considers to be the mission of the district, the objectives to be reached and the standards to be maintained; the manner in which the district is to perform these tasks, including the allocation of responsibilities and delegation of duties to specific staff members; and the methods to be used, the procedures to be followed and the reasoning to be applied in conducting the district's business, whether by the administration instructional staff, other employees, students, parents, or the public.

School board members have a variety of responsibilities. They sign an oath of responsibility as an agent of the state for the education of all children and youth of the state. They make decisions based on district policies and governmental regulations. School board members also seek to influence state and federal laws and regulations since these mandates often do not include needed funds for compliance, restrict local decision making, and interfere with existing successful programs. Board members also find themselves seeking adequate funds both at the state and federal level in order to support their schools. They attend workshops and seminars on a wide range of topics to enable them to make sound decisions. In some districts lots of time is spent listening to concerned citizens about issues of importance to them. It should also be noted that school board members as individuals have no authority. Their authority comes as a member of the board acting as the total group, unless an individual has been assigned some special authority on behalf of the entire Board. A school board is a corporate body and has power only during public meetings.

Generally, school boards are responsible for the admission, instruction, discipline, grading, and, as appropriate, classification of students attending the public schools in their district; for the employment and management of necessary professional and support staff; and for purchasing, leasing, maintaining, and insuring school buildings, properties, equipment, and supplies. Boards are also responsible for planning, setting policy and evaluating the results of the planning.

In some states school boards are one of the chartering entities authorized to receive and approve applications for charter schools. These schools can be proposed to operate within their respective school districts geographic boundaries, and the only charter entity authorized to receive and approve an applicant for the conversion of one of their existing public schools into a charter school is the local school board.

One of the most critical and important responsibilities of the board is to appoint a School Superintendent or the Chief Executive Officer to serve the district. Superintendents recommend actions for board approval and implement board decisions. The actual responsibilities of the superintendent may vary from state to state. In many states superintendents have powers and duties similar to those listed below taken from New York State Education Law 1711 (2).

1) To be the chief executive officer of the school district and the educational system, and to have the right to speak on all matters before the board, but not to vote.

2) To enforce all provisions of law and all rules and regulations relating to the management of the schools and other educational, social and recreational activities under the direction of the Board of Education.

3) To prepare the content of each course of study authorized by the Board of Education. The content of each course is submitted to the Board of Education for its approval and, when approved, the superintendent is responsible to see that such courses of study are used in the grades, classes and schools for which they were authorized.

4) Recommend suitable lists of textbooks to be used in the schools, subject to the approval of the Board of Education.
5) To have supervision and direction of all school personnel.
6) To have supervision and direction over the enforcement and observance of the courses of study, the examination and promotion of students, and overall other matters pertaining to playgrounds medical inspection, recreation and social center work, libraries, lectures, and all other educational activities under the management, direction and control of the Board of Education.

A national survey of relationships between superintendents and board members indicate that 93% of the superintendents surveyed indicated that they have a collaborative relationship with their Board of Education. Eighty eight percent feel that their board is effective. On the other hand 37% of the responding superintendents said they feel the amount of time spent on insignificant items consumes too much time and limits their effectiveness in what they would term "more significant items."

23% of Superintendents consider their Board of Education "not highly functional and effective."

In New York State 23% of the Superintendents consider their Board of Education "... not highly functional and effective." Twenty two percent of the Superintendents believe that their Board of Education "... does not act with a high degree of stability of mutual trust and respect." One third of them claim that the board works well together all the time.

Sixty percent said most of the time. School board presidents have indicated though that almost a third of them will not run for the board again. One board president was so upset with another board member she intentionally hit him with her car in the parking lot after a meeting. Board members yelling at each other and name calling are far more typical than the fist fights that have occurred at some board meetings. According to a five-state study conducted by the New England School Development Council, those school boards that are in constant conflict have schools that tend to have lower student test scores, fewer students going to college and more dropouts. Whereas high achieving districts had board members who worked as a team and had a strong understanding of crucial topics such as curriculum, testing and using data to monitor student progress.

Concern over school board members' behavior is not limited to school superintendents. At the 2008 Convention of the New York State School Boards Association delegates approved a Code of Conduct with sixteen guidelines on board behavior. Here is a sampling of some of the behavioral items mentioned.

a) Work with fellow board members in a spirit of harmony and cooperation in spite of differences of opinion that arise during vigorous debate of points at issue.

b) Base decisions upon available facts in each situation; to base each vote upon honest conviction unswayed by partisan bias, thereafter, to abide by and uphold the final majority decision of the board.

c) Communicate concerns and public reaction to board policies and school programs to the superintendent and other board members in a professional manner.

d) Keep confidential matters pertaining to the schools, which are legally required to be kept confidential and/or if disclosed, would needlessly injure individuals or the schools.

e) Strive to build and exercise a relationship with the superintendent that is constructive and positive and which enables district staff to function as effectively as possible.

f) Strive step by step toward ideal conditions for more effective school board service to our communities, in the spirit of teamwork and devotion to public education in a manner which serves as a role model to our students and which demonstrates that school board service is the greatest instrument for preservation and perpetuation of our representative democracy.

The complete document referenced above is located at www.nyssba.org

So what kinds of people serve on our school boards? The majority of school board members are white men age 50 or older. The largest share of board members, 46%, comes from business and professional backgrounds. While almost all board members are parents, only about half had children in school at the time of the survey. Board members are better educated and have higher incomes than most Americans. The mean length of service for school board members was 6.7 years, 41% had been in the post for from two to five years. School board presidents report that 64.2% of the districts turned over three or more of their superintendents in the past 10 years.

In terms of time commitment board members spend an average of 25 hours a month on board business, roughly one third of that time spent in board meetings. The time commitment is heavier in larger districts where nearly a fifth of the board members report spending more than 70 hours a month on the job.

More than three quarters of the school board members surveyed spent less than $1000 on their most recent elections. The biggest share of the money that was spent came from candidates and their families.

Only in large city school districts are board members compensated for their time and service.

CHAPTER TWO

Who Is The Enemy?

In this chapter we will look at the topic of who are the enemies of public education. It seems there are many today. We recognize that the word "enemy" is a very strong word. The definition for this word we are using is, "one who manifests hostility toward another." We could have chosen the word "foe" meaning "adversary," or even "antagonist" meaning "opponent" but will stay with enemy. We should clarify however that this word is not being used to describe any personal hostility but rather institutional hostility. The enemies that we have chosen to identify and include are: teachers unions with their 4.5 million members, some local boards of education and even state school board associations. The court system has also shown an adversarial relationship with schools in general. Some individual teachers and administrators in local districts could also be considered enemies of public education. The whole area of public school finance may also be viewed as an enemy by some. Perhaps the greatest enemy however is the **"apathy"** that is found in the general public.

Enemy #1
Teacher Unions

Let's talk first about the relationship of the teachers unions to our schools. It should be noted that these union organizations are made up of tens of thousands of individual teachers who give of themselves sacrificially day in and day out, year in and year out for the benefit of the children they serve. These are the heroes of the public school system. There is also no doubt that in the early days of education school leaders and the public took advantage of teachers who were willing to serve the children of the district. History clearly demonstrates the fact that teachers were significantly underpaid.

To compensate for some of the poor salaries, benefits were offered to teachers which included payment of health insurance and retirement plans. Teachers first became affiliated with unions in an attempt to enhance their working conditions, salary and benefits. All probably very noble reasons at the time.

Unfortunately when teachers come together under the banner of the teachers union the professional aspect of caring for the children seems to change.

Teacher contract salary increases are becoming too costly to support without some "giveback" in benefits.

As the years have past teachers salaries and benefits have continued to increase often at a rate much greater than increases granted in the private sector. Even in today's tough economic times teachers are being given annual increases ranging from three to five percent or more. The 2008 Teacher Contract Survey conducted by the New York State School Boards Association shows that the average teacher salary increase in the 2007-2008 school year was 4.2% The highest increase given to teachers by a district was 10%. In addition teachers continue to enjoy health insurance premium payments financed almost entirely by the taxpayers. This latest Survey shows that on average districts contribute 89.5% of the total Family Coverage Premium for health insurance. The average cost for this coverage is $13,889. This means that on average tax payers are paying $12,430 per teacher towards every teacher's health insurance. In addition 95.5% of the districts responding to the New York State School Boards Association 2008 Survey indicated they continue to provide health insurance to many retirees at district expense. One small district in Western New York has an ongoing annual liability of $12,000,000 to fund retirees' health insurance.

In addition to these benefits no one could deny that teacher's retirement plans are without question some of the most lucrative in the nation. For example, after 30 years of service some teachers can retire as early as age 55, with a State guaranteed pension of 60% of the average of the three highest years of their salary.

In 2008 Education Week, a nationally recognized weekly newspaper which deals with educational issues throughout the United States published Quality Counts 2008. In this special editorial project, teachers' salaries are reported from throughout the nation.

In New York State teacher salaries are reported to be at 100% parity when compared with salaries in comparable occupations.

In Pennsylvania teacher salaries are reported to be at 101.5% parity when compared with salaries in comparable occupations.

Some would be quick to point out that teachers work approximately nine months of the year, given their summers off and weeks off during Christmas, Winter and Spring breaks. A teacher in New York State worked an average of 181days with students in attendance during the 2007-2008 school year. Their total work year was 184 days. Some would further point out that teachers work primarily a seven hour work day and are paid additional money for all "extra-curricular" activities they choose to be involved in such as coaching a sports team or being an Advisor for a student club or activity. Granted some teachers spend longer hours and choose to be involved in other non-paying situations like the Parent Teachers Association.

An unbiased thinker would have to come to the conclusion that the days of teachers being under paid are long passed. In fact it may well be that it is time for communities to begin to take a much closer look at the salaries and benefits provided in today's teacher's contract. It certainly is time to begin to contain the escalating salaries as they are simply too costly for taxpayers to continue to support without some "giveback" in benefits.

"When school children start paying union dues that's when I'll start representing the interests of school children."

The organizations we are discussing in this section are actually two teachers unions in the United States. The National Education Association (NEA) has 3.2 million members, and receives a billion dollars annual dues income from its members. Membership includes teachers, paraprofessionals, school related personnel and higher education faculty. NEA has 50 state affiliates and more than 14,000 local affiliates. In the most recently reported period, 9/1/06–8/31/07, the NEA reported spending over $80 million on "Contributions, Gifts and Grants," nearly $49 million in "Representational Activities" $32 million in "Political Activities and Lobbying" and $21 million in "member litigation costs." The second union is the American Federation of Teachers (AFT) with 1.4 million members mostly in big cities, including New York City. AFT has 43 State affiliations and about 3,000 local affiliates. Membership includes teachers, paraprofessionals and school-related personnel, higher education faculty, nurses and other health-care professionals, local, state and federal employees and retired members. The AFT most recently reported spending $58 million on "Representational Activities," and $15 million on "Political Activities and Lobbying." According to a story in the Christian Science Monitor, August 24, 2005, The Misnamed National Education Association, Albert Shanker, one time President of the AFT was asked once whether he considered it part of the union's responsibility to improve educational quality. He replied, "When school children start paying union dues, that's when I'll start representing the interests of school children."

Common wisdom would say that because teachers are the direct purveyors of education they would be advocates for education. Unfortunately a review of history and present day practice tends to show otherwise. Sam Lambert, Executive Secretary of the National Educators Association told the National Educators Association Journal in December 1967, over 41 years ago, "The National Education Association will become a political power second to no other special interest group." Unfortunately Sam Lambert's prognostication has become reality. The strong influence, perhaps more accurately labeled domination can be found at the bargaining table and in the school board elections in most school districts.

Districts where school boards and its members stand up to teachers unions are the battleground for some of the most bitter and divisive politics in the nation. These districts also find themselves spending taxpayers' dollars defending their decisions in arbitration and the court system, when it should be used on better educational programs for children. Unions have deep pockets and think nothing of spending its "non-public" money on "...defending the rights of its membership." The National School Boards Association recently reported that while school board members say employees unions paid little more than 1% of their campaign costs more than half of the board members said teachers unions were, "active" and or "very active" in their elections.

Unions will stop at nothing until they occupy both sides of the negotiation table.

In an article entitled, The Union Label on the Ballot Box, Terry Mould says, "Teachers unions support 80 to 90% of the winning school board candidates." The unions will stop at nothing until they occupy both sides of the negotiation table. In other words teachers represent themselves and their interests on one side of the table and then have board members they have endorsed and supported on the other side of the table. In many cases teachers are becoming board members in the districts in which they reside. The law prohibits teachers from being on the Board of Education of the district in which they teach. Can a "teacher board member" really be unbiased when sitting at the negotiation table across from their peers? Particularly when during negotiations teachers always use salary comparisons from other districts to promote their need for salary increases to match those of the neighboring district? Some might even believe that encouraging more and more teachers to run for the local school board in their district of residence is a union strategy, and admittedly a great one at that.

More opposition to teachers' union assaults on democratic school boards needs to emerge in the future despite the feelings of futility. Unfortunately even the most effective school board members are vulnerable to reelection without union backing.

On an individual basis the majority of teachers really are advocates for the children in their school and want nothing but the very best for them. They are the true professionals. Teachers who are advocates for the students and their daily activities are often not likely to participate on union teams because they simply lack the time or interest to be involved in union shenanigans. Former Education Secretary Page states "The NEA and other belligerent teachers unions represent the most imposing barrier to academic school reform its reformers face today." As stated earlier, unfortunately when teachers come together under the banner of the teachers union the professional aspect of caring for the children seems to change. Various teachers told me:

"What I found most prevalent about the union meetings was how the retirees were the most vociferous representatives. The retirees never wanted to concede anything whether it was contract language or a dollar from the budget."

"Every district has teachers who stroll in late and leave as soon as the bell rings at the end of the day. These teachers don't prepare current lesson plans; they copy worksheets from 10 years ago. The end result is that these teachers often have a very high failure rate of children in their classes. Unfortunately these teachers get paid the same amount or more than others who might be considered outstanding teachers, which is an obvious fault in our pay system."

35

As a word of explanation it should be noted that salaries for teachers is generally based solely on years of service, earned degrees and college credit hours earned.

Some teachers went on to say, "It was disheartening to see that the union would rather see their least senior members without employment rather than compromise to the accommodations being suggested by the district." Sometimes this is referred to "...as eating your own."

"The teachers union is really little more than a political action committee advocating for the teacher's interests."

Several years ago the American School Board Journal ran a column which served to demonstrate that teachers unions weren't acting in good faith toward students and education policy and everybody knew it. The Oregon Education Association, a National Educational Association affiliate stated in their newsletter, "The major purpose of our association is not education; rather it is about the extension and or preservation of our members rites. We earnestly care about kids and learning, but that is secondary to other goals."

In 2007, lawmakers in Albany New York were given a powerful reminder of the political danger of going against union desires and initiatives. In this case a Democratic candidate who normally would be supported by the State's most powerful teachers union, New York State United Teachers, was rejected by the union for stating that he was in favor of school choice measures in the State. As a result the teachers union endorsed a Republican candidate in an important special election. The results of this special election could have possibly shifted the majority in the State Senate from its current Republican majority to a Democratic majority. One would have to conclude that unions are capable of anything and willing to do almost anything to influence legislators to uphold union positions on issues that are important to them. Payback to the union for it's endorsement of the Republican candidate occurred two weeks later. The Senate Republicans fast tracked a bill that would allow New York City teachers to retire with full benefits five years sooner than they previously could. The Democratic-led Assembly, which had already passed the early retirement bill last year, voted for it again and the Governor signed the bill. What a coup!

During the 2008 election season the state's most powerful teachers union, New York State United Teachers changed its official position and ended up providing an important endorsement for 35 state senators, most of who were up for re-election. Earlier in the year the union withheld its support from all lawmakers following a special legislative session in which the Republican led Senate backed a measure imposing an annual limit on property tax increases. The bill eventually died in the State Assembly, controlled by Democrats. The teachers union had opposed this bill because they were afraid of having an annual limit or cap on property taxes imposed by law as such a cap could limit their ability to negotiate higher teachers' salary increases in future contracts.

Two weeks prior to the 2008 election the teachers union extracted a commitment from 35 senators which stated that they would not support reductions in aid to schools if the Governor called the Legislature back after the election to deal with an announced $2.5 billion hole in the State budget. The current Senate Republican Majority Leader drew a clear line in the sand against the Governor's proposal of cutting school funding midyear. As a result of these endorsements the union backed senators received campaign donations, access to the union's sophisticated phone bank operation that uses computerized data banks to call thousands of voters a night and a sprawling field operation that helps candidates get voters to polling places on Election Day.

After the 2008 election Governor Paterson announced that the current State Budget deficit had risen by another $2 billion and budget cuts needed to be made. Over the next four years the state budget deficit is expected to be nearly $50 billion. In an earlier round of budget cutting in the Fall of 2008 education was spared although almost $1 billion in other cuts were made. This time the Governor indicated every area including education would be on the chopping block.

Prior to the actual recommended cuts even being formally announced union leaders made it clear that they were not budging. The New York State teacher union president stated, "I don't see any local leader wanting to come to the table to give something up."

The Rochester Democrat and Chronicle, a liberal leaning newspaper, usually supportive of teachers concluded in an Editorial, "It is the job of union bosses to look out for their members. But there comes a time when concessions become necessary. This is one of those times. People in the private sector are taking pay cuts and the salaries of others are being frozen. Still others are contributing more to their pension plans and health care costs. It's sheer lunacy for union leaders to expect their members to be treated differently from other sacrificing New Yorkers."

The very next day the Governor announced cuts in education totaling $840 million. Individual district cuts would range from 3% to 10%, depending on its level of State Aid and district wealth and needs. To manage these major cuts the Governor suggested that districts enact "substantial efficiencies" then dip into reserve funds which have been reported state-wide to be $940 million.

Only time will tell whether the teacher unions will grasp the severity of the economic situation and then be willing to contribute something toward the solution.

Teacher unions are also very involved with protecting the jobs and rights of unqualified teachers, particularly those that have received tenure. When school boards get involved in pursuing disciplinary issues against a tenured teacher taxpayer dollars really become an issue. A tenured teacher is a teacher who has served at least three years in a school district and has been granted what some refer to as "lifetime employment." Originally designed to ensure teachers were granted "due process when faced with dismissal," now tenure has evolved to the point where "in most states and school districts, tenure is not only easily obtained but losing it (and therefore losing employment even for cause,) is all but impossible." (Julie E. Coppice, A Tale of Two Approaches-The AFT, the NEA and NCLB, Peabody Journal of Education 80, no.2 (2005)

The costs to remove a tenured teacher run between $100,000 and $250,000.

Teacher disciplinary issues can range from a disagreement over the quality of the teacher's classroom work to issues involving allegations of child pornography or molestation. In New York State the costs to remove a tenured teacher is currently running between $100,000 and $250,000. These costs include not only the legal expenses, arbitration panel costs but also salary and benefits for the teacher while they are on paid leave during the entire time the process goes on. The entire process can take up to eighteen months to complete. Because of the personal nature of these actions the public very often never knows the final outcome other than the teacher disappears, and unfortunately in some cases reappears to teach in another district.

Teacher unions defend against attempts by a school board to discipline or remove a teacher stating they have a responsibility to support their members. Some times a teacher union representative will be candid enough to privately admit that defending the teacher really has no merit other than their responsibility to support their member.

How can action like this be justified when children and their education is involved?

According to press reports an English teacher in a Long Island district remains on the payroll and earns an annual salary of $113,559 even after pleading guilty to drunken driving charges, her fifth Driving While Intoxicated (DWI) arrest in seven years. She will remain on paid leave at least until a disciplinary hearing later this year. At the hearing an impartial arbitrator will decide whether she needs to be fired, despite a very likely prison sentence because of her drunken driving problems.

In New York City it often costs taxpayers $250,000 just to fire one incompetent teacher. Some teachers are convicted of serious felonies and still remain on the payroll, forcing districts to hold disciplinary hearings behind prison walls.

Finally in 2008 the New York State Legislature passed legislation that will automatically revoke the certification of teachers convicted of sex crimes against students. The law will end what is now often a yearlong administrative process during which the teacher continues to draw full salary and benefits.

The cost to taxpayers for teachers who are not in the classroom because of incompetence and wrongdoing is unbelievable. The cost to taxpayers in the nation's largest public school system, New York City, is estimated at $65 million a year, not including hiring substitutes or renting space for the so-called "rubber rooms" where accused teachers spend their workdays.

Accused of offenses ranging from excessive lateness to sex abuse, an average of 700 teachers at any given time read magazines, play cards and nap in the "rubber rooms." One teacher accused of sexually abusing a child has been assigned to a "rubber room" for 5 1/2 years. The average accused teacher waits four months for investigators to decide whether to bring formal charges. If they do, it takes an average of nine more months for a hearing and another six months for a decision. During this entire process the teacher draws their full salary and benefits at taxpayers expense. New York City employs 55,000 teachers. Only 10 teachers are dismissed annually.

School officials said teachers are pulled from classrooms only if evidence suggests they are a danger to children, and state laws and teachers contract rules make it difficult to speed the disciplinary process. One principal that had reportedly squeezed out a third of the teachers in his building who were not performing up to his standards was referred to by a union head as a "tyrant."

Good teaching really does make a difference.

Good teaching really does make a difference. The difference between a teacher in the 25th percentile (a very good teacher) and one at the 75th percentile (a not very good teacher) translates into a 10% out point difference in their students test scores. (As a frame of reference, on the Scholastic Aptitude Test, (SAT) 10% out points translates into an 80 point difference in raw test scores. With SAT scores being a major component of college acceptance obviously an 80 point difference in raw test scores can make the difference between a student gaining acceptance into the college of their choice, and in other instances acceptance into any college at all.

Teachers unions are not the only unions that defend their members in this way. The Liverpool Central School District near Syracuse, NY had two tenured administrators out on paid administrative leave for nearly a year at a total cost of $429,500. The cost of paying the two administrators continues to add up until the case is resolved which could take years, according to the lawyers involved in the case. The Liverpool Superintendent, Jan Matousek said, "It's not where the district would want to put its resources, but based on the way the State has put together the process, it's a very costly process." The administrators involved have filed a federal law suit attempting to get their jobs back under state and federal whistle-blower laws.

An issue that continues to be aggressively fought against by both teachers and administrators unions, although common practice in private industry is pay for performance. Human resource consultants, Hewitt Associates, recently reported that more than 90% of companies now offer some variable pay structure, up from 51% in 1991. Teaching is arguably the only profession in the country with ironclad job security and a well-honed hostility to measuring results.

At the 2008 NEA National Convention in Washington, DC the presidential nominee of the Democratic Party was loudly booed when he indicated his support for pay for performance. I believe teachers and administrators salary increases should be tied to student performance. What other business enterprise other than education gives set salary increases primarily for longevity, without any regard whatsoever to the recipients work or work product, namely student achievement? School districts in Texas and Colorado have finally been able to convince the majority of their teachers that pay for performance is not unreasonable.

For nearly twenty years I have been an advocate for pay for performance for everyone involved in education. Unfortunately it has been a difficult concept to negotiate with the labor unions. I think I have heard most of the "reasons" not to have pay for performance. These include:

"We don't trust the administration to be fair in the distribution of the dollars."

> *"Teachers are equal in ability and it would be unfair to have some teachers receive more money than others based on performance."*

> *"Teachers don't have control of which students are in their class so it isn't fair to tie their salary increases to student performance."*

The list goes on and on. It is interesting to me that similar conditions exist in a business environment, albeit with different descriptors, but employee salary adjustments are based on performance, at least to some degree.

Since teachers gauge student performance all the time through five, ten and twenty week reports as well as regular report cards, surely teachers can be evaluated as well, counters Gaynor McCown, executive director of The Teaching Commission, a bipartisan group in New York that works toward improving the quality of instruction. She wrote in a commentary: "If recognition of this sort is so troubling, divisive, and unfair, why do we continue to give grades to students? We give grades because they help us understand which areas need improvement and because they acknowledge superb effort and ability."

Houston Texas is the largest school district in the country to adopt a pay for performance plan for teachers that focuses on students' test scores. This plan offers teachers up to $3000 in extra pay if their students show improvement on state and national tests. At the Board meeting where this plan was unanimously adopted by the school board some teachers spoke against the plan claiming it was flawed. Other teachers and local business leaders spoke in support of the plan.

In Denver Colorado teachers can now sign up for a groundbreaking new pay plan that city voters endorsed by accepting $25 million in new property taxes. In other words taxpayers not only favored pay for performance for teachers they were willing to pay increased taxes in order to have it become a reality. A small group of teachers opposed the plan. They charged that the complex system was unfair to teachers who would have fewer opportunities to earn more money because of their assignments and for encouraging teachers to teach to the test.

While the emphasis on improved student test scores to attain the additional salary increases may be of concern to some, simply giving increases because one has worked another year or completed another graduate course should be of more concern. Some day, hopefully sooner than later, taxpayers will realize that while teachers and administrators should be adequately compensated, they also need to be accountable for their performance.

Isn't it time for school districts and teachers to start looking for professional ways like pay for performance, to provide appropriate compensation and leave the factory labor union model of the past behind?

Before leaving this discussion of unions as the enemy of public schools it would only be fair to acknowledge the teachers unions in many districts where they have worked cooperatively with school board and district administrators for the benefit of children and the local taxpayers. In most of these districts teachers have a genuine desire to serve the children and put their needs first. Generally the union leadership is also much less militant.

There is also a need to recognize that there exists the possibility of a teacher shortage in the next few years. Presently there are about 3.2 million people teaching in public schools in the United States. According to projections by researchers at the National Center for Educational Statistics school districts will need to recruit an additional 2.8 million teachers over the next eight years. The need is a result of baby-boomer retirement, growing student enrollment and staff turnover.

Between a quarter and a third of new teachers quit within the first three years on the job. Nearly 50% of the new teachers leave poor, urban schools within five years. Teacher Unions and their allies immediately point to "low pay, low status and soul crushing bureaucracies" as the main reason most new teachers leave the profession. The question is do the facts back up this claim? As I stated previously recent studies have shown that in New York and Pennsylvania teacher salaries are at 100% or more parity with comparable occupations. Conveniently forgotten in the teacher unions claims are the rich benefit packages teachers receive along with their comparable salaries. The benefit packages include primarily employee paid health insurance, probably the most lucrative pension in the State and a work year that is about 30% shorter than anyone in the private sector.

As I touched on earlier teachers also have the option of earning extra income by coaching athletic teams, advising student clubs and teaching summer school. All of this income financed at taxpayer expense. It should also be mentioned that in addition to regular negotiated pay increases that all members of the teachers bargaining unit receive teachers can individually add to their salary by taking a college course or in many cases involving themselves in professional development activities.

While a teacher shortage may be on the horizon across the country the fact is that in some areas there is lots of competition for any single position. It is not unusual to receive 500 or more applications for an elementary teaching position in a suburban school. On the other hand there is already an extreme shortage in specific areas like, math, science, special education and foreign languages.

To assist new teachers both New York and Pennsylvania State require mentoring programs. Pennsylvania also operates a State funded Teacher Induction Program and a Professional Development Program. Most teachers maintain that it takes perhaps two years to master the basics of class-room management and six to seven years to become a fully proficient teacher.

In the 1920's, 1950's, 1980's and very recently several states have experimented with merit pay or pay for perfor-mance. Teacher Unions are generally adamantly opposed to any of these concepts as a result of their position that all teachers should be treated equally. Hopefully more individual teachers will see what they are missing, not only personally but also how important these programs can be for the students and begin to urge their unions to support pay for performance. It is a concept that can work for the benefit of all.

As we conclude this important section on teachers and teachers unions let's review the qualities of a good teacher which hopefully will cause you to recall some of the great teachers you have had over the years that reflected these qualities. After a review of the research on this topic listed on the next page are some of the most commonly mentioned qualities. They are not listed in any particular order.

Qualities of a Good Teacher

1. Competence in the subject
2. Cares deeply about students and their success.
3. Possesses a distinctive character.
4. Teaches to the whole child
5. Is upbeat and positive
6. Not threatened by parent advocacy
7. Teacher really wants to be good
8. Takes risks
9. Willing to work long hours, many outside the classroom
10. Listens to their students
11. Are learners themselves
12. Have learned to self-analyze their teaching

Enemy #2
School Boards

Unfortunately another group that often ends up being an enemy to local public schools is the local school board itself. Mark Twain once said, "In the first place God made idiots. That was for practice. Then he made school boards." This comment is somewhat extreme but you get the idea.

Conflicts between the school superintendents and their boards of education have recently eroded many great educational initiatives in many school districts. In a recent survey of school superintendents conducted by the New York State Council of School Superintendents, nearly 29% of the boards of education were reported by their superintendents as "dysfunctional."

Unfortunately this is not a unique situation to New York State. In the February 2008 American School Board Journal Dr. Paul Houston the retired Executive Director of the American Association of School Administrators says this about the change that he has seen in board superintendent relationships. "I think we've moved in two directions at the same time. There's been a real deterioration in some ways and a strengthening that has occurred in others. There are some districts where you have first-rate board members who are working with the superintendent as a team. As for superintendents, despite what they may say around the coffee pot, a number of them feel good about their boards and how the boards have become more professional. At the same time, the relationship has become much more volatile. One or two bad board members can create a bad situation for the rest of the board. It's not professional and it's not appropriate, but you see a lot of that out there. Certainly you see it much more today than you did 30 years ago. I don't think there are bad boards. I think there are bad board members who create bad dynamics. And that poisons the well for everyone. When you become focused on getting rid of the high school principal or the football coach, then you end up with all kinds of troubles."

Examples abound nationwide to illustrate Dr. Houston's point. It was recently announced that the Oklahoma City school board had accepted the resignation of their superintendent after his being on-the-job for less than seven months. Prior to the resignation the board had directed the school district's attorney to conduct an investigation of the superintendent. Under the agreement worked out in conjunction with the resignation the superintendent will continue to be paid his full salary and health-insurance premiums for the next six months. In addition he received a lump-sum payment of $225,000 plus up to $30,000 reimbursement for legal fees.

In Kansas City Missouri the sitting school superintendent resigned. He agreed to step aside immediately but then he also agreed to stay on as a consultant through the end of the year, and presumably will receive full salary and benefits during this time. How could anyone looking at these two circumstances conclude that financial settlements in these situations were the best way to resolve differences among adults?

In Cleveland, Ohio there were eight superintendents in nine years. This "superintendent churn" only stopped when the mayor appointed the school board and hired a new superintendent.

In Miami-Dade County Florida the Board recently bought out the contract of their Superintendent at a cost of $368,000 in salary and benefits. This is the same superintendent that the board waged an intense campaign to woo and win to the job just four years ago. In response to his buy-out the Superintendent stated, "A fair analysis of this is that I didn't run in the political lane, out of preference for running in the academic lane." During his tenure the graduation rate inched up and thousands more students took Advanced Placement classes.

In a 2006 survey of School Board Presidents nearly 63% reported turnover of 3 or more superintendents in the past ten years in their districts.

Talented superintendents will stay clear of districts with difficult boards. Working for a district with such a board can be career suicide for some superintendents.

School board members do not always act with a high degree of civility, mutual trust and respect.

In New York State a sitting Superintendent had his contract extended an additional year at the final Board meeting in June. This re-established his total contract duration to three years. At the first meeting in July, less than 30 days later, one newly elected Board member led an effort to have the Superintendent resign. In fact, he requested that the Superintendent resign at that meeting. The Superintendent refused. It is worth noting the newly elected board member was a previous administrator in the district who had been forced to resign several years earlier. For many years after he resigned he continued to offer himself as an interim candidate for nearly every administrative position that became available. Various sitting board members encouraged the superintendent not to even consider hiring this person. Eventually he was elected to the board and the situation described above occurred as a result.

Over the next several months this single Board member brought embarrassment not only to himself, the Board of Education, the Superintendent but to the entire school community. On numerous occasions at public meetings the Board member would put his finger within inches of the Superintendent's nose and say, "I will see that you are gone!"

Within a few months this Board member convinced a majority of the Board to hire an attorney to begin an investigation of the Superintendent. Allegations were brought by this Board member and other Board members who had been undermining various actions of the Superintendent, despite the approval of the majority of the Board. Teacher union leaders also abetted the investigation. After several months and over $50,000 spent in public funds for the investigation, the allegations were shown to be without merit. During this time however the entire district was disrupted, particularly student achievement. In the end a financial settlement was reached between the Superintendent and the Board of Education. The real losers in this case were the local taxpayers who paid nearly $300,000 to settle the matter that really involved a "vengeance factor" of a minority of the Board members.

Perhaps there are reasons why 22% of the Superintendents responding to the New York State Council of School Superintendents survey indicated they believe their boards do not act with a high degree of civility, mutual trust and respect.

Based on the circumstances just related one might wonder about the fact that a critical area of oversight responsibility for the Board of Education is that of school finances. Individual school districts are responsible for having an independent auditor audit the district books. Unfortunately this limited oversight has proved to be insufficient. For example in the Roslyn Union Free School District near New York City both the School Superintendent and the Assistant Superintendent for Business ended up serving extended jail time for improper and illegal use of district funds. Millions of dollars were misappropriated or misused for personal purposes even though the Board of Education had fiscal oversight.

As a direct result of this and other serious illegal personal use of public money many states have begun regular financial audits to be conducted by state government. In New

York State former Comptroller Alan Hevessey stated in 2005, "I believe approximately one third of the school districts have excellent financial procedures and controls in place. Approximately one third need minor tweaks in their financial procedures and controls and approximately one third of the school districts need a major overhaul of their financial procedures and controls." As a result all school districts in the State are being audited by the Comptroller's Office on a three year rotation. Today, more than three years after the Comptroller's initial statement the results of audits conducted by his office appear to correctly reflect his forecast. It is however regrettable to note that the Comptroller himself was subsequently forced to resign as a direct result of his misuse of public funds for person gain.

Unfortunately examples of questionable use of public funds continue. In one district a shared fuel facility was utilized by various local governments including the school district. The Comptroller's audit reported that there were no locks on the fuel pumps, no records of which agencies pumped fuel from the pumps and no one could assure the auditors that fuel was not in fact taken by individual employees for their personal use.

In Wake County North Carolina a fake invoice scam operated for at least two years before being discovered. It is estimated that this scam cost the district $3.8 million. District employees created purchase orders for transportation department equipment. The dollar amounts of these orders were below bidding limits so they could be channeled to a particular motor supply company without review.

By prior arrangement, the supplier never delivered the equipment. District staff, however, allowed payments to be made. Portions of the fraudulent proceeds were then distributed to the corrupt district employees and the balance kept by the motor company workers. Four district employees and two motor supply house employees were sentenced to prison.

In one of the largest school districts in the State of New York a voter approved $119.5 million capital project was supposed to be completed four years ago. As of this writing it is still not completed and is currently over budget by $2.5 million. Auditors wrote "... completion of the project will almost certainly exceed the current cost of approximately $122 million." The district paid $267,000 for musical risers and wheel chair lifts that were never used and were placed in storage at a cost of $2640 a year. The district approved $1.7 million in payments for the capital project without assurance from the architect that the work had been properly performed. In the Fall of 2008 there was actually a delay in opening school as clips that hold walls and ceilings together were never installed thus creating an extremely dangerous situation. Installation of the clips in several buildings impacted could not be completed in time to allow for a safe opening of school and the opening had to be delayed.

The auditors report also states that there were 2400 change orders issued because of "inadequate planning and poor communication between the district and the contractor." According to State Education Law all change orders over $20,000 are to be approved by the board. Auditors found however officials had purposefully split the orders into smaller amounts to avoid Board oversight. The audit also found that of 144 orders that did exceed $20,000, only six were approved by the Board.

In another section of the Comptroller's Report it is indicated that two employees of the district were paid $51,000 in severance packages. Retirement incentives of $45,000 were paid to two officials who were not eligible for the payments and an administrator was given an additional 51 sick days valued at $25,000. None of these cash payments were approved by the Board of Education as required by Law.

In response to press reports on this matter, one tax payer said, "Government bodies waste more money than anyone. I would like to see criminal charges against former Board of Education members and district officials, if they are warranted."

In 2008 New York State Attorney General Andrew Cuomo asked 48 school districts in Westchester County for detailed information on how they pay their lawyers as part of an investigation into potential abuse of the State pension system. At issue is whether lawyers who worked for firms hired by schools were also being listed as school employees and as a result getting individual pension benefits at taxpayer expense to which they were not entitled? Since the initial investigation it has been determined that several lawyers have been inappropriately listed as school employees ultimately making them eligible for retirement benefits. In one case the Attorney General alleged that an attorney had fraudulently collected "in excess of $700,000 in taxpayer-funded pension benefits." The Attorney General later investigated all school districts in New York State. The Federal Bureau of Investigation, the Internal Revenue Service as well as the Attorney General all launched criminal investigations that could result in felony charges being upheld in Court.

All of the above questionable, if not illegal activities and actions occurred without the appropriate and legally required supervision of the individual Board of Education. These are extreme examples of a failure on the part of these Boards to fulfill their fiduciary responsibilities.

Nepotism, favoritism shown to relatives, can be another huge issue in some school districts. In one district in Pennsylvania 50 of its 310 faculty and staff were directly related to board members.

In a number of national studies superintendents relationships with school boards were found to be a decisive element of superintendent tenure. Often, conflict with the school board is cited as a common reason for superintendents leaving a district. Many superintendents could relate various stories of school board members who wanted to get involved in micromanaging the day-to-day operations of the school. Here's one example.

The district was arranging to buy a new tractor. The superintendent and business manager brought information to a board meeting explaining the specifications on the tractor along with the financial information. Prior to the next scheduled board meeting, one of the board members visited area dealerships and received information on a number of different models of tractors. He came to the next board meeting with all the information and further proceeded to tell the superintendent and the Board of Education what tractor should be purchased and which dealer it should be purchased from. Obviously this is not an area where board members should be involved. Administrative details should be left to the administration.

In another example a superintendent explained that one of the board members in his district received information from the public about a staff member. The Board member did not like the specific style or way that a certain staff member was doing things. He called the staff member on the phone and subsequently threatened to fire the employee. Obviously a situation like this can cause major conflict between other board members and the superintendent. As an individual, board members have no power to make these decisions and should not be involved in personnel matters in this manner. Unfortunately sometimes board members lose sight of their role as an individual on the board. This can be caused by perceived power, hidden agendas, or a dislike for the superintendent or other members of the board.

In one district when the consultant asked what steps the board was taking to keep its partnership with the superintendent positive and solid, four of the seven board members made it very clear that they did not see this as the boards concern. Unfortunately, this hands-off attitude is not all that uncommon among board members, for two main reasons.

1) Many school board members feel more committed to dealing with the needs and interests of particular constituencies than to the concept of the board as a "corporate governing" entity. This anti-team attitude obviously goes against the idea of the board's collective accountability for building a solid working relationship with its superintendent or for governing.

2) The inherently adversarial and limited view of the school board as responsible for "watching the critters so they don't steal the store." This probably comes with the legislative turf, but is still fairly common. When board members basically see their primary role as standing back and judging administrative performance rather than the idea of taking the initiative in building a solid partnership with the superintendent the superintendent will feel alienated. After all, adversaries are not naturally partners, not without a lot of hard work.

On the contrary high-impact school boards explicitly and formally take responsibility for building and maintaining productive and positive professional relationships with their superintendents, often by incorporating this commitment into their "governing mission."

Maybe the State of Hawaii has it right. There are no school boards in Hawaii. King Kamehameha III created the atypical school governing system in 1840. As the school system grew it was handed over to the state education department and has remained under the state's jurisdiction ever since. This is difficult for the population even though Hawaii is a small state. The state education department is responsible for all the typical school board activities, including the determination of the time and date of graduation. Can you imagine needing a change in a bus route schedule and making the phone call to the State Education Department requesting this change?

Almost 14 years ago, Boston University took over the management of the Chelsea, Mass. School system. Chelsea's Board of Education was so crippled by crime and corruption that it could no longer function. Board members were being accused of everything from nepotism to organized crime.

It would be extremely unfair to leave this section on local School Boards as an "Enemy" of public education without also acknowledging the great work of many individual school board members and boards in general. Here are three examples.

In a school district in New York's Southern Tier the school district was looking to provide a new lighted athletic complex for students playing soccer and baseball. A parent in the district convinced his employer, a major highway construction company to donate the use of several large pieces of highway construction equipment to the district to make the playing fields a reality. This same parent convinced his fellow employees, many heavy equipment operators, to donate their time on weekends to operate the company donated equipment. Few, if any of them even lived in the district but freely committed to the work. The local Board of Education President donated all the diesel fuel necessary to operate this heavy equipment throughout the entire time of construction. This amounted to a gift of several thousands of dollars. As a result this school district now has what has been described as "... the finest natural grass athletic complex in the Southern Tier."

Then there is Richard A. Moss who was first asked to run for his local Ohio district's school board in the mid-1950's. He recently marked his 50th year as a school board President of his district in Northeast Ohio. At 91 he is believed to be the longest serving school board president in the United States. Mr. Moss described his school board experience as "... a wonderful experience." Mr. Moss retired from the school board in 2008.

Here is one final example of stellar school board service. Dr. William J. Brennan, recently retired president of the Ticonderoga Central School Board of Education and 2008 winner of the New York State School Boards Association's top award for distinguished service. Dr. Brennan served on the board for 40 years. First elected to the board in 1968 Dr. Brennan served as president for 33 years and was a member of the district's finance, facilities and shared decision making committees. He helped lead the district through six major building projects, the annexation of a neighboring school district, and has helped guide 12 different superintendents during his tenure.

Enemy #3
School Board Associations

Before leaving the topic of school boards there needs to be some discussion of the State School Board Associations, to which most local school districts belong. The associations are generally member-driven associations who claim to serve school boards by providing advocacy, information and programs. In reality often these Associations have become just another political entity to be contended with. They become involved in educational policy formation, influencing educational finance priorities and political activity based on relationships primarily in the State capital. The associations often find themselves wrestling with questions of whose interest do they represent, specific areas of the state, powerful groups or individuals, like their own Board of Directors, local school boards or all the children throughout the State?

For example delegates at the 2007 Annual Business Meeting of the New York State School Boards Association (NYSSBA) which represents nearly 700 school boards and more than 5,000 school board members in the state passed the following resolution:

"RESOLVED, that the New York State School Boards Association create a statewide task force that will explore and formulate ways for school districts to contain costs."

The report from this task force was published one year later in 2008. It is important to keep in mind that the purpose of the task force was to "… explore and formulate ways for school districts to contain costs." The Task Force developed 55 recommendations. An analysis of the recommendations however shows clearly that the group failed to achieve their stated purpose. Only 5% of the recommendations actually dealt with cost containment. Here is a breakdown of the 55 recommendations into categories I have created.

CATEGORY	# OF RECOMMENDATIONS
Contain Costs	3
Increase State Aid	8
Transfer costs to State	8
Existing Power	3
Existing Authority	4
State Legislation required	12
State Legislation and union support required	4
Change State Regulations	7
Create more Task Forces	4
No action indicated	2

Without detailing every single recommendation, as that is not the purpose of referencing this report, let me provide a flavor of what is involved in each category and a reaction to the various recommendations.

Cost Containment

In the area of cost containment one of the three recommendations is "… there would be no new legislative mandates without a complete accounting of the fiscal impact."

This is a great recommendation even if it is one that has been circulated many times previously and fallen on the deaf ears of the legislators for over ten years.

Increase State Aid

There are eight different recommendations I have listed under this category. One states, "BOCES aid to school districts should be extended to all BOCES-operated summer programs to encourage year round learning." Without debating the educational merits of this recommendation, the cost implications would be huge. How does such a proposal serve the stated purpose of the report "to contain costs?" Presently most summer programs are either optional or cost neutral.

Transfer Costs to State

One recommendation in this category reads, "The State should assume the employee pension costs entirely and relieve employer contributions…"

Acceptance of this recommendation would contain costs at the school district level, in fact it would reduce costs at the school district level, but how does a transfer of district costs to the State save taxpayers money?

Existing Power

Local school districts currently have the power to negotiate all the recommendations in this category. One of three recommendations is, "Require school district employees to contribute … toward the cost of health insurance."

Local districts, through its Board of Education already have the authority to require health insurance contributions from its employees. The Board simply needs to be willing to negotiate with its bargaining units to get this "give back" from the unions. This is certainly not an easily obtained contract item but the authority exists for it to be obtained locally.

Existing Authority

Local districts already have the authority to bring about the four recommendations in this category. One is, "Increase incentives for health insurance buy-outs."

Districts have the authority to do this now through the collective bargaining process. Many unions have already agreed to a provision for this in the existing contracts. The local districts simply need to negotiate a larger incentive.

State Legislative action required.

The report contains twelve recommendations in this category. One states, "Change the state law that reimburses school districts the following year for approved preschool programs in the current school year." Obviously this has financial implications for the State, particularly in the current economic climate. The recommendation in no way is a measure of cost containment for the taxpayer it simply shifts the burden.

State Legislative action and union support required.

Four recommendations are proposed in the report in this category. One states, "Amend the Triborough provision of the Taylor Law to exclude teacher step and lane increments from continuation until new contracts are negotiated."

It is simply not realistic to ever think that unions are going to support this legislative change. It is also not realistic to imagine that the legislature is going to pass such legislation in light of the fact that teachers' unions are the largest contributors to the campaigns of the sitting legislators.

Change State Regulations

The report contains seven recommendations in this area. One states, "Establish uniform statewide assessing standards." This recommendation proposes abolishment of the 1,128 independent assessing jurisdictions in the State which causes a lack of statewide assessment standards. This is a wonderful idea. The problem is it will not happen. What is the point of even offering a recommendation that is doomed to failure from the outset? Wouldn't it be more productive to propose recommendations that have at least some likelihood of becoming reality?

Create more Task Forces

Four recommendations are made in the report to create additional Task Forces. These would deal with such topics as "Streamlining Mandates," Fiscally Dependent School Districts," "Special Education" and "Innovation in Education."

Creating more task forces completely fails, in my judgment, to contribute to a meaningful and productive discussion of ways for school districts to contain costs

This brief analysis clearly demonstrates that the Task Force members' solution was to put the responsibility for cost containment in most cases on someone else. This happened in at least 42% of the recommendations. Making the matter even more ridiculous is the fact that the "someone else" is primarily state legislators and bureaucrats, people that have failed to demonstrate a past record of success in getting things done.

To move from a stated goal of cost containment to simply recommending in nearly 30% of their recommendations that some other group, specifically a larger group of taxpayers pick up the costs is outrageous. Furthermore, although it was not part of the Task Force's initial scope of their work, wouldn't it have been nice to have them include *some* potential cost reductions?

Reflecting local community values is difficult for a State Association.

The financial crisis which became front page news in New York State after the 2008 elections was noted earlier in this chapter. To repeat briefly, Governor Paterson announced that the current State Budget deficit had risen by another $2 billion and budget cuts needed to be made. Over the next four years the state budget deficit is expected to be nearly $50 billion. In an earlier round of budget cutting in the Fall of 2008 education was spared although almost $1 billion in other cuts were made. This time the Governor indicated every area including education would be on the chopping block.

Subsequently the Governor announced cuts in education totaling $840 million. Individual district cuts would range from 3% to 10%, depending on its level of State Aid, district wealth and needs. To manage these major cuts the Governor suggested that districts enact "substantial efficiencies" then dip into reserve funds which have been reported state-wide to be $940 million.

Timothy G. Kramer, Executive Director of the New York State School Boards Association reacted with these comments. "The state is obviously facing a serious financial crisis, but mid-year school aid cuts would force school districts to make devastating cuts that hurt children. While the Governor has suggested that school districts use reserve funds to weather any mid-year cuts, such action would leave school districts with absolutely no safety net in the coming year, when the state faces an estimated $12.5 billion deficit. Local property taxes would likely skyrocket in 2009 just to maintain existing educational programs. We will work with the State Legislature to reject these proposed school aid cuts."

"We will not entertain the possibility of cuts in anything. Just give us the money you promised."

This statement is consistent with the recommendations from the School Boards Task Force cited previously. Unfortunately the consistent message is, we will not entertain the possibility of cuts in anything. Just give us the money you promised.

How can reasonable people continue to promote this type of message in the financial crisis our country is currently in?

The state associations also sometimes act in an adversarial manner to local school boards and the district administrators. One of the important responsibilities of the local Board is to be reflective of the values and belief system of the local community. Some time ago the New York State School Boards Association passed the following resolutions:

"We encourage school boards to invite discussions among students, parents, staff and the community regarding hatred and bigotry based on race, ethnicity, gender, sexual orientation, disability and religion which endanger the pluralistic and diversity principles for which this nation stands.

We encourage school boards to involve students, parents, staff and the community in developing and supporting education which invites understanding and acceptance of other's differences which aim to eradicate hatred and bigotry."

Yet, despite a total US population of less than 3% gay and lesbian the State Associations are not hesitant to promote

65

resolutions like these to their membership that encourage school boards to invite discussion of "sexual orientation" and "acceptance of differences," words known in many circles as words used to promote the gay and lesbian agenda and life style.

In its 2008 Position Statements NYSSBA, under the section entitled NYSSBA Leadership Responsibilities #3 states, "NYSSBA should take a leadership role in encouraging school boards to develop successful strategies for integrating respect for cultural differences into the educational experience. In carrying out this mission NYSSBA shall:

a) Encourage school boards to ensure that the importance of respecting others who are unique and different because of racial, ethnic, gender, sexual orientation, disability and religiously related reasons is part of the curriculum.

b) Encourage school boards to invite discussion among students, parents, staff and the community regarding how hatred and bigotry based on race, ethnicity, gender, sexual orientation, disability and religion endanger the pluralistic and diversity principles for which this nation stands.

Experience would clearly demonstrate also that on issues of religion particularly, State School Board Associations are notorious for pushing extreme separation of church and state positions.

The First Amendment to the United States Constitution declares "Congress shall make no law respecting an establishment of religion or prohibiting the free exercise thereof or abridging the freedom of speech or of the press." Thomas Jefferson indicated it was his belief that "...by guarding in the same sentence and under the same words the freedom of religion, of speech, and of the press anyone who violated any of these issues throws down the sanctuary which covers the other."

The Framers of the U.S. Constitution understood quite clearly that religious freedom is one of the most fundamental human rights that exist. After all, religious freedom is the main aspiration that sent America's founders searching for independence from England. This is also why the Framers included free exercise of religion in the First Amendment to the United States Constitution.

Why would State School Board Associations not be more concerned about protecting fundamental rights to exercise religion held by perhaps 95% of the population than they are about promoting understanding of sexual orientation and acceptance of differences held by less than 3% of the population?

State School Board Associations also find themselves closely intertwined with other associations such as State Superintendents groups and State Parent Teachers Organization associations who in their eagerness to be part of the state political apparatus lose sight of their unique mission.

Most State School Board Associations are also very hesitant to get involved with a local board which may be publicly dysfunctional for fear of losing the districts membership dues. This is very unfortunate because there have been instances where an offer of mediation by the State Association could have made a significant difference.

Enemy #4
The Court System and Judges

Our court systems and some judges have at times demonstrated disastrous results when it comes to their relationship with schools and administrators.

Judge's irresponsible actions cost taxpayers several thousands of dollars forcing a school district to defend itself and its' Superintendent in an action in which the judge had no jurisdiction.

An example of the negative and costly influence of the court systems was demonstrated in the Cattaraugus County Court in the Southern Tier of New York State a few years ago. In this case a judge was tipped off in some way (some believe perhaps by a local school board member who was looking to tarnish the reputation of his School Superintendent) that a local school district had "...failed to deliver the required testing to a classified student within the district." This alleged omission first came to light when a Deputy Sheriff appeared in the office of the School Superintendent at approximately 11:00 am one morning to deliver a subpoena. The subpoena ordered the superintendent to appear in the Judge's court room by two o'clock that afternoon. After consultations with the school district's attorney, whose offices were more than three hours away from the school district, and a request from the school district's attorney to the Judge for a postponement of the hearing which was denied, arrangements were made for a local attorney to accompany the School Superintendent to the Hearing.

During the Hearing the Judge ordered the Superintendent to have the test completed on the student and report to the court when it had been done. The Judge also indicated he was holding the Superintendent in "contempt of court for his actions" and stated he "... would hold the Superintendent personally responsible for a fine of $1000 a day until the testing results were delivered to the Judge.

The school district's attorney was again consulted and he concluded that under the Education Law the Judge did not have the right to order the testing done.

With the approval of the Board of Education, it was decided that the testing should be completed anyway in order to protect the Superintendent from the ongoing fines that were mounting up on a daily basis. The testing on the student was completed within a week. The results of the tests showed that the student did not require any additional services from the school district.

In the meantime an appeal was filed by the school district in the New York State Appellate Division Court. This court supervises the Cattaraugus County Court. After several weeks the Appellate Court reversed the decision of the Cattaraugus County Judge. This court determined that the Judge did not have jurisdiction in this matter as the district had maintained throughout. The Appellate Court also removed the imposition of the fines and suggested that perhaps the action against the Superintendent was actually vengeance of some kind.

This Judge and the court system he represented was an enemy of the school district as well as the Superintendent. His irresponsible actions cost the taxpayers of the district several thousand dollars to defend an action in which the judge had no jurisdiction. The personal impact on the superintendent was also significant.

Fortunately such disastrous results as these are not always the case.

"Bong Hits 4 Jesus"

In 2007 the United States Supreme Court ruled in favor of schools and administrators in the case over a student's display of a banner reading, "Bong Hits 4 Jesus." In this case which goes back to 2002 students at Juneau Douglas High School in Juneau, Alaska were dismissed from class to view the passing of an Olympic torch relay outside the school. During the event the principal of the school noticed a banner which read "Bong Hits 4 Jesus" and asked students to fold it up. When they refused her request she removed the banner from their possession. The principals' action was based on the existing school board policy against pro-drug messages. The case eventually found its way to the U.S. Supreme Court as a First Amendment issue. The student claimed that his First Amendment rights of his free speech had been limited by the action of the principal.

In a split decision the court ruled that schools have the authority to regulate drug related messages on public school campuses, "The special characteristics of the school environment and the governmental interest in stopping student drug abuse allow schools to restrict student expression that they reasonably regard as promoting illegal drug use," Chief Justice John G. Roberts said in the majority opinion for the court. This was the first major ruling in two decades on student speech by the U.S. Supreme Court.

Courts at a lower level have also been helpful to schools but not always in their initial decision.

In Monroe County, the county that includes Rochester, New York, school districts have benefited since 1985 by receiving a percentage of the county sales tax as part of their revenue stream. These districts together are the county's largest employer with over 21,000 employees and a total budget of $1.7 billion. In 2008 in order to balance the county budget where there was a major shortfall in revenues, the county manager, with the support of the Republican majority in the county legislature, decided to keep all of the sales tax revenues for themselves rather than sharing a portion of the sales tax revenue with the school districts. This decision was made one night in December halfway through the school year without any warning to the area school districts. This action by the county created an immediate cut in revenue of $14 million for the school districts. In 2009 the total revenue cut would have amounted to $29 million. Districts had no time to plan for the loss or even lobby against the action. Subsequent to the County's decision school districts joined together and filed suit against the County in County Court. This County Court ruled that the County of Monroe did indeed have the authority to stop the sharing arrangement that had been ongoing for 23 years and keep the money it held back to balance its own budget.

This decision was appealed to the New York State Appellate Division Court who reversed the County Court decision and found in favor of the school districts and against the County of Monroe. The County then appealed to the New York Supreme Court. The highest Court in New York State sustained the position of the school districts. The County of Monroe lost. If the County had prevailed the schools would have lost a major revenue stream without warning or the opportunity to plan for the loss. In a disturbing and costly move on the part of the impacted school districts they agreed to allow the County of Monroe to repay them the lost revenue over a period of years rather than as a lump payment. As a result the County has in essence borrowed the money from the school districts and their taxpayers. Since when are school districts or more correctly school district taxpayers in the banking business of lending money, and lending it interest free at that?

The school districts and the County have expended thousands of taxpayer dollars in legal fees and costs to finally resolve the issue. Taxpayers again are the real losers.

Enemy #5
School Administrators

Unfortunately sometimes even school administrators can be viewed as enemies of the very institution they are appointed to care for. Or, at least as an enemy of the people they are appointed to oversee, teachers, support staff and students.

In one case a federal district judge in California ruled that a California teacher had a right to display banners in his public school classroom with such slogans as "In God We Trust," "One Nation Under God," and "God Bless America."

Judge Roger T. Benitez of the U.S. District Court in San Diego rejected a motion by the Poway Unified School District and other defendants to dismiss a lawsuit filed by the teacher Bradley Johnson.

Mr. Johnson, whose suit said he had hung some of the banners for as long as 25 years in his classroom at Westview High School, was told by his principal in 2007 to remove the banners because they conveyed "a Judeo-Christian view-point," according to court papers. The teacher sued on First Amendment free-speech grounds.

Judge Benitez said in the September 4, 2008 opinion based on the teacher's alleged facts, which the judge must accept as true at this stage in the legal process, the 33,000-student Poway district had created a limited forum at the school in which teachers have free-speech rights. The school district has permitted other teachers to display posters with Buddhist and Islamic messages, and "Tibetan prayer flags," the suit contends.

The judge said he did not view Mr. Johnson's banners as communicating a religious message. "Rather the banners communicate fundamental political messages and celebrate important American shared historical experiences," he said.

The court rejected the district's arguments that the banners could be regulated because the teacher is a government employee and any classroom speech is part of his job duties.

In another case involving a student, Erica Corder, a high school valedictorian in the Lewis Palmer School District in Colorado, was forced to publicly apologize for sharing her Christian faith during a 30-second message at graduation. Erica was chosen as one of fifteen valedictorians to each give a 30-second message at their graduation in 2006. Each valedictorian orally presented a proposed speech to the principal before graduation.

At graduation, Erica delivered a different speech that expressed her faith in Jesus Christ. After the ceremony she was escorted to see the assistant principal, who said she could receive her diploma only if she apologized to the entire school community.

Under duress, Erica prepared a statement saying the message was her own and was not endorsed by the principal. The principal, Mr. Brewer insisted that she include the words, "I realize that, had I asked ahead of time, I would not have been allowed to say what I did." Erica complied because she feared the school would withhold her diploma, as had been threatened. She was also afraid that the school would put disciplinary notes in her file and would generate negative publicity, which could prevent her from obtaining her goal of becoming a school teacher. Principal Brewer sent Erica's coerced statement in an email to the entire high school community.

One might rightly conclude that the student was wrong to deliver a graduation message which was different from the one she orally presented to the principal. One might even assert that she should be punished for this behavior but the question needs to be asked, "Did the school district or the

Principal specifically have a right to coerce the student to speak against her will when she was no longer a student?"

Students do not shed their right to free speech when they stand at the graduation podium.

CHAPTER THREE

Apathy, Frustration and Fear

The title of this book, "The Sin of Apathy" was not chosen lightly or without reason. Apathy is defined in *The American Heritage Dictionary of the English Language* as, "Lack of emotion or feeling," or "Lack of interest in things, indifference." Apathy is not only found in the public school system. It permeates the general public's attitude in many areas including government enterprise.

Mathew D. Staver, Founder and President of Liberty Counsel states in his landmark book, <u>Eternal Vigilance</u>, Broadman & Holman Publishers, 2005, "I have learned that we lose our religious liberties for three primary reasons: (1) ignorance of the law, (2) hostility toward religion, and (3) apathy.

In the March 3, 2008 edition of *Newsweek*, Chuck Colson, President Richard Nixon special counsel and now a respected author and speaker states, "It is a sin in my opinion not to be involved in your civic duty."

As mentioned previously there are approximately 56 million children that attend public schools in the United States. Nearly $500 billion is spent annually in the educational enterprise. Despite these facts, schools are constantly pleading for more parental involvement. Many Parent

Teacher Organizations cease to exist due to lack of interest. Attendance at parent teacher conferences, particularly at the middle and high school level has diminished significantly. School budgets and school board elections generally draw 10% or less of the eligible voters.

The primary mission of the Teaching and Learning Institute (TLI) is "To increase the number of candidates who are willing to run for their local school board." The Institute is especially interested in working with candidates who are committed to family values based on a traditional Judeo-Christian belief system. Our work is much more difficult than was ever expected.

Our organization has spent thousands of dollars in advertising on television, radio and newspapers, as sponsors of various community sporting events and other youth activities. Hundreds of hours have been spent contacting churches and other groups we thought might share our concerns and interest. Some individuals have stepped forward to indicate their interest in becoming a candidate and to request our help.

There should be a great deal more concern however about the enormous amount of apathy that is demonstrated by most people. Our experience has been that when we explain our mission most people are supportive of it. Translating any of that support however to any degree of action has been very difficult.

Apathy abounds in terms of meaningful involvement in our public school.

People are quick to complain about a situation in their school or one they have heard about. When it comes to being motivated to doing anything about some of the situations that they describe so passionately, however the motivation or actions are simply not there. Admittedly people are extremely busy and there are far too many demands and opportunities available. Isn't their inaction really part of being apathetic however, at least on the issue of public schools?

Unfortunately sometimes even well known national radio personalities, including some "Christian personalities" are quick to put down the public school system nationwide for its "sins and shortcomings." In addition to being counterproductive and hurtful such condemnation devalues those teachers and administrators who are Christians who have chosen to work in the public school system as their vocation or place of ministry.

During the months involved in writing this book the working title, "The Sin of Apathy" was mentioned to several people. Some people reacted to the title indicating they believed that many people are not really apathetic but rather frustrated and in some cases actually afraid.

In these conversations people recalled many instances where their frustration level accelerated to the point of feeling entirely helpless. Most examples centered on school budgets and school building projects or issues where they simply felt they "...had not been heard" or their "...comments appearing not to have value." In other conversations people mentioned the fear factor. Fear of not knowing enough to participate, fear of retribution to their children, fear for their business or other interests in the community may also be factors. Previous negative behavior of the Board of Education or specific members of the Board can also be cause for people to fear becoming involved in such a potentially negative environment.

Let's look at each of these concerns of apathy, frustration and fear in more detail.

One area of extreme disappointment we have experienced has been the response of evangelical church leaders. Over the last three years TLI has been in contact with several hundred churches in an attempt to make them aware of the opportunity for service on their local school board by their members and attendees.

We have offered printed materials for distribution, formal and informal presentations and personal conversation. To date the number of churches who have responded in anyway to these offers has been minimal.

If it was discernable that these churches or their members were doing anything about the "terrible circumstances in the public school" they often describe, that would be one thing. The fact appears to be that the best solution they can come up with is to remain apathetic and complain, decide to home school their children or place them in a church school.

Any of these solutions is certainly a right and choice anyone can make. These solutions don't resolve the issue for the millions of children who still remain in the public schools. In fact removing and separating children and families who support and encourage strong morals and ethics based on Judeo-Christian values actually hurts the public school system and the children who remain. The children who are left lose all the value of "salt and light" that Jesus spoke about in the New Testament. Some very practical aspects of this loss are the loss of positive modeling of ethical behavior, proper interpersonal relationships as well as how to live life in a challenging world.

The choice to remain apathetic about meaningful involvement in our public schools also does nothing to improve the situation for anyone.

Let's turn now to the issue of people's frustration. There are plenty of justifiable reasons to be frustrated with all levels of government, not just our schools.

There may be other reasons besides frustration but certainly at least one indication of frustration with schools is the fact that in New York State less than 10% of eligible voters take the time to vote in May. On one single day in May voters have the opportunity to vote on their local school budget and school board candidates. Less than one in ten eligible voters voted.

What are some of the possible reasons for frustration? I think some statements made by various people indicate some of the reasons.

"It doesn't matter, taxes go up anyway."

"I don't think it matters whether I vote or not."

"I'm not aware of what is going on in the district."
If the budget is defeated in the first vote, the Board simply puts it up for a revote."

"I get to vote on the budget but I have no say as to how the money is spent."

"My vote doesn't really matter. The 'school people' do whatever they want to do."

"The teacher's unions can determine the outcome of the election and the budget vote by simply getting their members and family members to vote."

"School finance is so complicated no one can understand it anyway."

"The current members of the school board manipulate the election process so that the people they want on the board get elected."

"I received a good education when I was in school and my children seem to be doing all right so why should I take the time to vote."

"Schools are just like other forms of government. The 'little guy' like me can't really make any difference in the way things are done."

Voter turnout appears to correlate to what is going on in the district.

Historically voter turnout in a district appears to be correlated to what is going on the district. When the community is happy or complacent with the results and decisions of the school leaders, voter turnout declines. Voters appear to trust the school leaders and remove themselves from the interactions and importance of sustained involvement.

On the other hand when community members are upset over an issue such as an announcement of a proposed major property tax increase, a personnel decision like the failure to reappoint a popular coach or a change in a popular curriculum area they demonstrate their concern. In some districts voter turnout doubles or triples when there is an issue of this kind in the background.

In an effort to increase voter participation a few years ago the New York Legislature passed a law that required that all schools vote on the same day in May. In New Jersey low voter turnout became a major part of the rationale to move school voting day from April to the November general elections. Pennsylvania voters already vote on school issues at the same time as the November general elections.

Maybe the only motivation that will ultimately succeed in getting voters more involved is the current trend of increasing local property taxes at a rate that voters simply conclude is too much. Over the last couple of years more and more taxpayers have begun talking about the need to "… relive the Boston Tea Party." For those too young to remember this reference let me explain. This was a time in our history when people in New England became so tired of the oppression of the British they dumped all the tea on the boats in the Boston Harbor into the ocean.

Some taxpayers are so tired of the way current elected officials are handling issues they believe it is time to turn all the elected officials out. Based on the results of the 2008 national and state elections it appears the "tea party" has not yet begun in earnest but it may be on the way.

During 2008 a Commission appointed by the New York State Legislature recommended the imposition of a property tax cap. Nearly 80% of taxpayers surveyed supported this recommendation. As most taxpayers would expect teacher unions, school administrator groups and most school boards voiced their opposition to such a cap. Teacher unions went so far as to promise to campaign against the re-election of any legislator who voted in favor of the tax cap. As of the writing of this book tax cap legislation has passed in the Republican controlled Senate but has not even been officially considered in the Democrat controlled Assembly.

Finally let's turn to the possibility that people fail to get involved in their public school system because of fear. Some people have stated that they don't get involved in schools because they are afraid to get hurt. One story is told of a candidate for school board candidate who faced opposition from some members in the community because she had publicly challenged the status quo. Upon her election she found herself regularly in the eye of nearly every storm that developed in the district.

Some people are afraid that teachers and other school employees will take it out on their children if they say anything that could be interpreted as negative toward them. Some people who may own small businesses or are dependent on community members for their livelihood may be concerned that by taking a stand on an issue that may be unpopular in the community their business or livelihood will be negatively affected.

Jon Meacham a columnist for Newsweek magazine recently opined, "It takes guts to offer oneself for election, and serve. It is far easier to throw spitballs from the stands than it is to seek and hold office."

So what is the solution for the lack of involvement? Here's one that was proposed recently on a blog in response to another news story about the failure of the school board to provide adequate oversight .

"Get rid of the elected school board and go to having them appointed by the Town Supervisor or Mayor. Then ONE person is accountable and not a group of part time people that only serve 2 years and all point fingers at each other. Boards of education have proven themselves to be worthless in containing the empire building fantasies of school superintendents. Most boards are made up of parents and retired teachers – they should be made up of accountants and lawyers. Maybe we need to get rid of the superintendents "cabinet" and all of those fancy administrative titles and replace them with an elected and paid oversight board."

While I appreciate the candor and thought behind this response I find several problems with it.

1) A board appointed by the Town Supervisor or Mayor takes away an important part of local control, namely the opportunity for local voters to directly elect people they want to control the local education enterprise. Appointment of board members could have the potential to make the board even more political than it can be now.

2) While there are situations where "Boards of education have proven themselves to be worthless in containing the empire building fantasies of school superintendents" thankfully this is true in very few

situations. Having the superintendent accountable only to the Mayor doesn't seem to provide any safe guard from "empire building."

3) I share the bloggers concern about the fact that more and more boards of education are comprised of retired teachers. I am even more concerned about the increasing number of current teachers who are being elected to serve on school boards. This situation makes impartiality and separation from self-interest very difficult. I don't understand or agree with the bloggers concern about parents being on the boards of education. It seems to me that parents are important stakeholders in the education enterprise, especially because they have children involved in learning and most of the parents are also taxpayers. While accountants and lawyers do make thoughtful and articulate board members and some of them should be involved, I don't believe that they should dominate the make up of any board. For that matter no professional group should dominate a board. A diverse board can be an excellent board.

4) I agree with the blogger that districts do need to be aware of the number and costs of administrators involved in the district, this awareness both from a need and cost basis.

5) In the situations I am aware of where board members are paid for their services it appears that they tend to have the feeling that they need to earn their pay by being overly involved. This often leads to micro managing and becomes burdensome rather than helpful for everyone involved.

CHAPTER FOUR

Involvement is not a Dirty Word

Earlier parts of this book have sometimes portrayed the public school system and many of the entities and people involved in the system as scheming, self indulgent, power hungry, ruthless, politically motivated and downright dishonest. So as we move to the next section of the book, specifically designed to interest readers to consider becoming involved in this system that has been portrayed so negatively, it becomes my job to help you turn the corner, or actually to turn the ensuing pages so you can see the opportunities and needs of the public school system through a more positive lens. I recognize the magnitude of the task.

To have you turn the corner with me and see the opportunities and needs of the system could be a daunting task except for one reason. Simply put that reason is **children.** In fact 56 million children. Beyond the children what are some other significant reasons to get involved in our public school system? The answer to this question can be approached in several ways including from a biblical perspective.

The New Testament clearly demonstrates that Jesus Christ certainly was political. Although he was not a member of any political party and did not hold any official position of power, Jesus challenged the corruption, hypocrisy and injustice in which He lived. As His followers, can we do anything less? If we see Jesus Christ as an example for us, how can we sit back and allow others to dictate how the world around us should be. Jesus was involved in transforming the world. He modeled servant leadership. He was humble and He associated with people of the world and yet kept His priorities straight. He has set a great example for us to follow. We need to get involved!

The Scripture also teaches us there are really two kingdoms in which we live. The Kingdom of God and the Kingdom of this World. We live in this world. We are part of this world. We need to take an active role in our world as Christians. There are specific Scriptures that speak to these issues. They are:

"Let us not become weary in doing good, for at the proper time we will reap a harvest if we do not give up." Galatians 6:9

Or as Jesus prayed to His Heavenly Father in John 17: 15, "My prayer is not that you take them out of the world but that you protect them from the evil one. They are not of the world even as I am not of it."

"You are the salt of the earth. But if the salt loses its saltiness, how can it be salty again. It is no longer good for anything, except to be thrown out and trampled by men. You are the light of the world. A city on a hill cannot be hidden. Neither do people light a lamp and put it under a bowl. Instead they put it on its stand, and it gives light to everyone in the house. In the same way, let your light shine before men, that they may see your good deeds and praise your Father in Heaven." Matthew 5: 13 - 16.

Some people have suggested that "people of faith" abandon the public school system. At times they have even said that its "hard to ignore the fact that government schools are destroying our children intellectually morally and spiritually." I find this statement unconscionable.

As mentioned earlier a small segment of members of the Southern Baptist Church have proposed that their denomination establish an exit strategy for removing all of the children of the Southern Baptist denomination from the public school system. Research shows that if all Christian students were withdrawn from the public school system, 50 million children currently in the system would still remain. Don't we as Christians have a responsibility for these 50 million children who would remain in the public school system even if we withdrew all of our Christian children? How can one be salt and light in the world if we become separated from the world and are not part of the world?

Dr. Jerry L. Schmalenberger, former President of Pacific Lutheran Seminary in Berkeley, Ca., in a sermon entitled, *When Christians Quarrel* maintains, "It is unthinkable that a Christian would not vote! It is unthinkable that Christians would not run for public office! It is unthinkable that Christians would withdraw from the responsibility of taking part in public life. The Christian has a responsibility to Caesar for all the privileges which the rule of Caesar brings. We are citizens of this world and must be good ones, if we are Christ's disciples."

Some have said that politics is a dirty game and if we participate in the political environment it will compromise those of us who are involved. Such a statement would indicate that the person making that statement really doesn't understand what politics is all about. The American Heritage Dictionary defines "politics" as "The art or science of political government. The conducting of or engaging in political affairs." Politics is indeed about compromise. It can also be dirty. The question remains, "Does it have to be?"

The public school system is very complicated. In some places it is filled with questionable practices, shady people and dishonoring behavior, but not everywhere, probably not where you live. When making negative statements and assertions about public schools in general, as some Christian leaders are prone to do, one needs to be careful not to denigrate the good work, and in many places the great work, being done by many God fearing people in hundreds of school districts across our great country. Many teachers, administrators and support staff see the public school as their "mission" field. This is a good thing!

It would be our hope that by now you the reader would be at least curious enough to wonder about becoming involved in your local public school and how you could develop an approach to become involved that could prove to be meaningful and wouldn't be filled with frustration?

For readers who have reached this point here are some ways we have developed just for you.

Nine Ways to Become Involved in the Public School System

1) Attend school board meetings in your community to find out what the Board of Education is doing. A telephone call to the District Clerk's Office in the district will enable you to find out when and where the next meeting of the board is to be held.

2) Once you get a sense of the issues the board is working on, request the opportunity to speak to the board about the issues that are of interest to you, or on which you have an opinion. The District Clerk

can tell you the proper protocol to gain the opportunity to speak to the board.

3) Shortly after the beginning of school the board and administration will be working on construction of the next year's proposed school budget. Ask for copies of draft budgets as they become available and offer constructive suggestions regarding the budget.

4) Consider writing a Letter to the Editor of your local newspaper outlining your thoughts on an issue the board is currently dealing with. Be sure the tenor of the letter is positive and constructive.

5) When the school district is looking for volunteers for committees, planning teams etc. make a call to the superintendent's secretary to let the district know you are willing to serve in these capacities.

6) Read the district newsletter, if one is distributed to keep up-to-date on what's going on in the district.

7) Join the local Parent Teacher Association or Parent Teacher Organization (PTA or PTO), attend their meetings and consider becoming an officer of the group.

8) Offer to be a volunteer in your school. This may involve such activities as tutoring a student, working in the library or helping in the cafeteria.

9) Always present yourself as a positive person, looking to encourage the good things that are going on in the district, not a "negative" person who finds fault with everything.

If you have already been involved or prefer to jump in deeper here are some thoughts on becoming a school board member.

Eric Randall, a spokesman for the New York State School Boards Association said, "School board service is certainly not for the faint hearted. It's a demanding role and it's very important. If truth in advertising laws were strictly enforced it might more accurately be called fool hearty. Has anybody ever told you you'd be great in a high stress job in which you don't get paid, you have to sit through endless meetings discussing such fascinating topics as state aid formulas and energy efficiency studies? By the way, in this job some people would probably grow to hate you. On the positive side you'd know that your decisions could affect hundreds of lives every day and far into the future. Some school board members seem to have the intestinal fortitude or something to last several terms others however have had enough after one term."

"School board service is certainly not for the faint hearted."

Certainly there are many and varied reasons for school board members to leave after serving for a short time. The hours can be long and often inconvenient. There can be piles of paperwork or e-mail documents to be studied and acted on. Butting heads with administrators, unions and parent's groups, each with their own agenda can become hurtful as well as frustrating. Personality conflicts and public criticism often come with the responsibility. Millions in tax payer dollars figure into the mix of responsibilities however. A former board president said "If people knew what they're getting themselves into when they were running for school board, no one would run." Another challenger for a board seat, suggested with tongue in cheek, "I must be suffering from dementia to even consider running." Let's hope that's not true.

The Teaching and Learning Institute conducted a survey of current and retired school board members. In the survey we asked a series of questions about their board service. The first question was:

What initially motivated you to have an interest in running for the school board?

Russell Leberman an eight year board member in the Avon Central School District said, "Our district was in a financial crisis and it was suggested to me that my combination of teaching experience, involvement in the schools, and some financial experience would make me a good candidate. I also wanted to donate my time to public service in a forum that I felt the Lord could use me."

Phil Jones a multi-term board member in the Arkport Central School District said in answer to the question simply, "Five children."

Bill Roeske, an eleven year board member in the Belfast Central School District said, "Several members of my community approached me and encouraged me to run for the vacant school board seat. They thought I could provide representation from the area. I went ahead and ran in the next election. We had two children enrolled in the district at the time."

Rev. Bruce Ellis, who is currently serving as a school board member in the Forestville Central School District said "The school district is the largest employer and most influential organization in our community. As a believer in Christ I felt obligated to bring His love and light through the school doors."

In response to the same question regarding his motivation to run for the board in Franklinville Central School District Richard Hughes said, "A Christian friend was on the board and he was looking for another Christian to serve on the board with him." Hughes has now completed 18 years on the Board.

Janice Dalbo of the West Seneca Central School District says "My husband and I were convinced that to be an effective Christian in our community required my involvement. I am a professional educator and felt that serving on our school board would be one way I could use my training and experience to help the kids of our town."

Ray Martel of the Nunda Dalton School District said his election to the Board gave him an opportunity to make a positive change in the direction of the school.

Finally Dr. Edna Howard a long term board member indicated "As an educator at both the elementary secondary and college level I wanted to support educational growth of older children in my School District."

These same individuals also shared their concerns about running for the school board. Their concerns were indicated by the following statements.

"I was not a native or born in the community. I was concerned whether I would indeed be accepted in the community."

"I was concerned that opposition from some interest groups who might negatively use my profession of faith as a reason for me not to serve. There were small efforts in this regard but none had any impact on the outcome."

"My inexperience and time commitment involved. I was concerned with any political fallout harming the reputation of our church since I was a pastor in the community."

"One concern was having enough exposure and electability."

"Enough people need to know you and respect you and to have enough confidence in you to vote for you."

"I was concerned about the opposition because I was running against a local banker who was much better known in the community than I was."

"The board of my district at the time was under fire for some poor budget planning. The district was looking at a major tax increase. Also the administration at the time had an adversarial stance on teachers and the community. Decisions were being made 'top down' and confidence in the Administration was lacking."

Another concern expressed when considering a run for the board by one survey respondent was:

"I was concerned that my children might pay the price if teachers and/or administrators didn't approve of a position that I took as a board member."

These are all legitimate concerns and demonstrate the level of thought that goes into making an important decision about running for the Board of Education. The good news unquestionably is that hundreds, perhaps thousands of children in these various school districts benefited from the decision of these individuals to become a school board candidate and ultimately a school board member.

Other interesting results of our survey included the facts that 75% of the respondents had school-age children in the district when they originally ran for the Board of Education and it should be added, all survived.

Eighty-eight percent of the people surveyed were elected to the board the first time they were a candidate.

Our survey also asked this question. "Were there times when your Judeo-Christian ethics and morals impacted decisions that you were making on the board?"

One currently serving board member said, "I'm presently working with the high school principal to begin a process of offering a Bible as literature elective in our English department. I know there will be resistance in various areas as this issue is contentious."

Another respondent said, "We opened each meeting with prayer. I was asked to do this."

Someone else said, "One area I can think of was in the selection of some textbooks. I did have an opportunity to look at some of the proposed books and put in a word for good family values."

In the area of student discipline, this same board member said, "For the most part we had great teachers and a principal who did a good job. I was always pleased when I could support right and just discipline by the principal."

Another respondent stated, "It was always a pleasure when I could promote the idea of the value of each individual. This seemed to help foster an atmosphere of trust, respect and teamwork. My service also gave me an opportunity to influence moral decision-making. For example, within the first year of service the board elected me as vice chair and the business manager specifically asked if I could be placed on the school's accounts for the purpose of signing checks in our double signature check signing system."

Another board member responded, "I felt my personal Judeo-Christian ethics and morals were brought to life when we had opportunity to give some people a second chance. Also when I could show respect for others and their opinions." On the other hand, "In one particular case, when a very popular coach was charged with driving while intoxicated I was able to take a firm stand against us supporting her return as the coach." In a similar personnel matter a first year teacher/coach reportedly took team members to "Hooters", an area bar, had a few beers and drove the team member's home in a school owned vehicle. When confronted the coach admitted his "failure" but was dismissed from his position as a teacher and coach without a second chance. All board members supported this decision.

Another board member responding to the survey stated, "I had influence in the consideration of Christmas music and celebrations. Our teachers as a group were given a green light in these areas. In the area of sex education, I insisted that parents have full access to curriculum and that they were aware of their option to have their children withdraw from certain parts of the curriculum if they chose to do that. I also advocated for no condom distribution in schools and that no representatives of Planned Parenthood or any of their initiatives be allowed in our school at any time. On the other hand,

I encouraged public and parent forums on topics like drugs and alcohol."

A previous board member stated, "I was able to advocate for the approval of a Bible club session in the high school, and was able to utilize faculty advisors for this purpose."

Several board members indicated their concern about the problems facing school districts and their students in regard to proper use of the Internet. All districts are required to have an Acceptable Use Policy in connection with computer usage. Development and the ongoing updating of this document is an area that will continue to benefit from the input, wisdom and guidance of board members with strong Judeo-Christian ethics and morals. Decisions in the area of Internet usage can have lasting value for all students as well as faculty and staff.

CHAPTER FIVE

What Does the School Board Do?

A member of the Board of Education works together with other board members and the administration to create a shared vision for the school district. They are also responsible for establishing district goals and priorities and with the oversight of the general operation of the school district.

Several years ago many organizations including schools followed the advice of organizational development people and spent a great deal of time developing a Vision and Mission Statement for the school district. While these statements should be reviewed and perhaps tweaked occasionally a complete rewrite of them seems unnecessary and perhaps a waste of time in most cases.

Goals, objectives and priorities of the district are items that should be updated annually. Often board members and members of the administration set aside time in the summer to review the past years progress towards previously agreed upon goals and objectives. Then they establish new measureable goals and objectives. Many districts choose to hold a retreat to accomplish this important work. Such a time together gives a concentrated period of time for this unique and important purpose apart from the normal operation of the district. Often this time together also serves as a time to develop a team approach to problem solving. This can prove to be beneficial throughout the school year.

The Board with the input from the Superintendent is also responsible for setting the general direction for academic programs, public relations, facilities and employee bargaining unit contracts. An important responsibility is that of deciding which courses will be offered to students. For example the Superintendent may have been made aware by the High School Principal or the Director of Curriculum and Instruction that student enrollment in Business subject courses is noticeably declining. He may also be aware that student interest in more computer or technology courses is increasing. The Superintendent in this case would make a recommendation to the Board about either moving teaching staff to accommodate changing course offerings or recommending the termination of some teachers in the Business area and hiring other teachers who are certified to teach in the computer/technology areas. These actions require Board of Education approval.

The Board of Education has responsibility to approve all labor contracts.

Another very important responsibility of the Board of Education is to ratify or approve all contracts with the various employee bargaining units within the district. While the official contracts are actually written between the Superintendent of Schools and the bargaining unit the final approval of the contract falls to the Board. This fact is sometimes conveniently forgotten by school boards. Frequently one will hear school board members bemoaning the fact that a major cause of budget increases is due to the escalating salary and benefit costs negotiated by the unions of the district. What school board members often conveniently forget is that they or their predecessors are the ones who ratified the contracts that contained those escalated salary and benefit costs.

In most districts when it comes time to begin negotiations of employee contracts the Superintendent meets with the Board of Education to receive from them some guidelines that are to be followed during the negotiation process. During the negotiations the Superintendent continues to update the board on progress and if necessary asks for changes in the guidelines that have been given to him. Once the contract negotiations are complete and the proposed contract has been approved by the bargaining unit then the Board has the opportunity to approve or disapprove the contract. With salary and benefits comprising between 75 and 80% of the total expenditures in any school budget the final outcome of contract negotiation is critical to controlling the escalating costs of school budgets in any district.

Salary and benefit costs are only part of the overall budget that is developed each school year in every district. How districts actually develop their budget differs somewhat by the leadership style of the Superintendent and the desire of the Board of Education.

There are at least six principle approaches to budgeting: incremental budgeting: line item budgeting: program budgeting: the planning, programming and budgeting system (PPBS): zero-based budgeting: and site-based budgeting.

1) **Incremental budgeting** has traditionally been the most common budgetary technique used by school districts. In this system the previous year's budget is used as the baseline for the new budget. Adjustments are made through percentage increases applied to the budget as a whole. State legislators often use an incremental budgeting process because it is simple

and easy to explain to the general public. The disadvantage of incremental budgeting is that the current conditions are considered only minimally and no evaluation of past performance is required.

2) **Line item budgeting** like incremental budgeting relies on previous budgets for starting point data. It differs from incremental budgeting in that each line in the budget receives individual consideration. Percentage increases or decreases may be applied to one or more lines of the budget. The objective of the expenditure becomes the focus of attention. The disadvantage of this system is a strong tendency to perpetuate the status quo.

3) **Program budgeting** organizes the budget by the major functions of the district often using State required budget codes. The function may then be linked back to an individual who has organizational or fiscal responsibility. Though the superintendent and board remain in control of the final decisions regarding the budget, program budgeting provides for greater input from staff and the community than line item or incremental budgeting.

4) **Planning, Programming and Budgeting System (PPBS)** links the budgeting process to programs through planning evaluation processes integrated into the systems. The process is highly complex, requiring both sophisticated technology and highly trained individuals for successful implementation. Its impact may be seen in the current emphasis on establishing goals, measuring progress toward those goals, and using the information obtained in the development of future budgets.

5) **Zero-based budgeting** is based on the premise that each year's budget starts with zero and is built anew with justification for the inclusion of each item. The

budget is developed through the use of decision packages that specify program goals and outcomes and the consequences of alternative funding levels. These decision packages are then ranked in order of importance. Generally speaking, there will be two groupings of decision packages 1) those that are mandated by statute required for basic operation and 2) discretionary packages. This author prefers the zero based budgeting approach as it has been extremely helpful in controlling costs and limiting the status quo in budgeting.

6) **Site based budgeting** enables staff members in schools and school systems to engage in decision-making regarding the expenditure of funds. This process commonly begins with revenue projections and allocations to program areas and buildings by the superintendent and board. Each building decision-making committee develops goals and objectives for the building and a budget designed to meet those goals within the parameters provided by the administration and board. Site based budgeting has many advantages, including building staff's sense of responsibility for and control over their funds. There is a danger however, that those building budget managers varying levels of skill will result in inequities both in funding and in the wise use of funds.

A school budget year runs from July 1 through June 30 of the following year. Often the next school budget is developed beginning in December or January of the current school year. Depending on the approach used by the Superintendent, he and other members of the administrative staff will often prepare budget drafts which are then given to the Board of Education for review and input.

These drafts ultimately are finalized and approved by the Board of Education for submission or presentation to the community. In New York State the public vote on the budget takes place the third Tuesday in May. Assuming that the budget is approved by a majority of the voters within the district the new budget goes into effect on July 1.

Without any doubt the most important role that the Board of Education plays in any school district is the actual hiring of the Superintendent of Schools. Candidates considered for the position of Superintendent are generally highly educated, highly qualified individuals who have many years of experience in education. They also tend to be compensated very well. Their salaries are still much lower than Chief Executive Officer (CEO) salaries in many companies with comparable budgets, or in major non-profit organizations.

Superintendents of Schools are expected to be available to a wide variety of constituents 24/7, 365 days of the year.

There is generally a small pool of people both willing and qualified to take the very high profile position of Superintendent of Schools. They function as the Chief Executive Officer dealing with ever-changing laws, often changing boards, mandates, curriculum, challenging union leaders and positions, parents with a wide variety of expectations for their children and thousands of taxpayers who are having a very difficult time justifying the increases in school taxes. Superintendents must be available 24/7 to deal with these issues. They are also ultimately held responsible for everything that occurs in the school district.

The primary responsibility of the Superintendent is to provide educational leadership to the district under the guidance and supervision of the Board of Education. Generally the Superintendent is granted an employment contract of a minimum of three years and a maximum of five years which is mutually agreed upon by the Superintendent and the Board of Education. The Board is responsible for the overall supervision of the Superintendent and for an annual performance evaluation. In some districts conducting this evaluation has proven to be somewhat awkward and difficult to perform. In these cases board members feel uneasy about evaluating what they might refer to as "the educational expert." This became such an issue in some states that legislation was passed that requires boards to evaluate their Superintendent at least annually. This is a good thing! While not required by law it is also a good thing for the Board to conduct an annual Board Evaluation and ask the Superintendent for input on the Board's performance from his perspective as the CEO.

The final responsibility of a Board of Education member to be mentioned here is the need to show respect for other board members, members of the administration as well as community members. Previously we have discussed the lack of respect shown in certain instances to fellow board members and members of the administration. Unfortunately there are also too many cases on record where board members have not shown appropriate respect to community members who in fact pay all the bills.

Most community members feel somewhat uncomfortable and may be even threatened when they address school officials. They are often not familiar with school culture and vocabulary and view school personnel as the "experts." Their feelings could be equated with challenging a decision their medical doctor was about to make on a health issue.

Most people have only the experience of being a student in a school to draw on in terms of their familiarity with school culture and vocabulary. Sometimes out of frustration for their lack of understanding community members show their frustrations by the words they say, the volume level at which they speak the words, and the way they person-alize their comments. Board members should recognize the responsibility they have in these circumstances to be patient, encouraging and respectful of the community members.

CHAPTER SIX

Prepare Your Mind for Action

P repare your mind for action but make sure the action you are proposing and your motives for those actions are appropriate. The goals of the Teaching and Learning Institute are twofold.

1) To increase the awareness of what is happening with local school boards of education and to learn the Boards areas of responsibility.

2) To increase the number of quality candidates that choose to run for a seat on their local school board who are committed to family values based on a traditional Judeo-Christian belief system.

During the years we have been involved in this important work we have also found ourselves discouraging some people from considering becoming a candidate for their school board. As a result we have developed a list of reasons *not* to run for school board. Let's take a look at these reasons.

1) Personal Issues
Unfortunately some people who consider running for their school board are really only concerned about some

single issue that really affects their child or a member of their family.

One woman we talked with was not pleased with the current placement of her daughter who was a classified student in special education. She wanted a different placement for her. No one in the district would agree to the placement the mother wanted. During our conversation I realized that she had certainly taken her desire for a change of placement for her daughter through all the appropriate channels and in the appropriate manner. I applauded her efforts in that regard. Unfortunately she believed that by gaining a seat on the school board she could get what she wanted for her daughter. I assured her that based on my experience that would not necessarily be the case. I also reminded her that even if she was able to accomplish her single goal she would have committed herself to a multiyear term on the Board where many other items probably not of real interest to her would require her time and effort. She ultimately agreed that running for the Board in an attempt to get an "appropriate" placement for her daughter was probably not a good idea. She came to a very wise conclusion.

2) Disagreement with an Administrator

Another common reason people give for running for the Board is that they have had a serious difference of opinion with an administrator. Often the disagreement centers on some disciplinary action that was taken by the administrator in regard to the person's son or daughter. They believe that getting on the Board will give them the opportunity to somehow "discipline" or perhaps more accurately "get even" with the administrator in question. This is not a productive way to deal with such an issue.

Certainly differences of opinions occur between students, parents and administrators and in some cases administrators are wrong. I recall one instance when a parent adamantly disagreed with the discipline measures that had been administered to her son by the high school principal. In various meetings the principal and the Superintendent of Schools had referred to the District's Code of Conduct for Students in pointing out the infractions. The student was guilty of the infractions outlined by the Principal and the discipline measures called for in the Code had been properly enforced. Despite these circumstances the parent continued to feel her son had been inappropriately wronged. (It is also worth noting that in this case the student had accepted the disciplinary measures and moved on.) This "injustice" became the motivation for the mother to consider a run for the school board.

3) A "stepping stone" to a political career

Sometimes potential school board candidates are looking to begin a political career and decide to use the school board as a stepping stone to a career as a county, state or even national elected official. In many areas of public life would be politicians do use "entry" level positions as stepping stones. Given the complexity of the issues that school boards deal with, the financial implications of the issues and the obvious benefits of multi year service at this level, using school board service as a means to fulfilling higher political ambitions is unfortunate, perhaps even unwise.

4) Serious time constraints

A question one needs to seriously ask if thinking about becoming a school board member is, "Do I have the available time to properly prepare for the meetings and the time to attend the meetings and other related functions?" So, what is the time commitment needed to be a productive school board member? Board members are expected to attend all meetings of the board. Regular school board meetings are held at least once a month. In some districts meetings take place twice a month. It is not unusual for these meetings to take three or more hours each. Many boards have a committee system which require attendance at these meetings as well. Board members should also be prepared to take time to read board packets, gather information, listen to community concerns, and study new laws/issues and programs.

The amount of time devoted to board work by individual board members varies widely. In an Illinois survey, few board members reported spending more than 30 hours each month on their board duties. A majority said they spend 10 to 20 hours on board work each month. The New York State School Board Association indicates that the average time commitment of Board members in New York State is 6 hours per week.

Service on the Board of Education takes time and effort.

There is also an expectation that board members will attend various school functions such as National Honor Society events, sporting events, School Board Association meetings as well as Graduation and students music programs and activities. At a minimum anyone contemplating serving on a board of education should plan to spend six to ten hours a week so engaged. One Board member in the Southern Tier of New York State commented, "It's lots of work. There are a lot of hours involved. I attend about five board functions a month, including committee meetings and workshops. I put in at least 10 – 15 hours every week on my school board duties."

Serving on a school board does take time and energy however most board members find that with a little planning and organizing on their part the necessary time is available. Some board members find they must re-order other priorities in their life. Some have to cut back on their hobbies. Others find they have less time to relax or watch television. A few find they must ask their employers for released time.

5) Unwilling to participate in training

Becoming a well prepared, knowledgeable Board member requires not only a major time commitment but a willingness to participate in training and board development activities. Unfortunately some new board members believe they know enough when they begin their Board service that they don't need training. This attitude can serve as a destructive force on the Board and to the district. Unfortunately there are far too many examples of this happening.

Many states now require new Board members to participate in mandatory training, particularly in the area of finance. Similar to the medical field, education has its own vocabulary, jargon and methods for conducting business. Any candidate for a school board position who believes she can serve the children of the district, the local tax payers and the board itself effectively without training, is not only extremely arrogant but is simply demonstrating a serious misunderstanding of the responsibilities and complexities of the position. "A successful business woman a good board member does not necessarily make."

6) An open mind is essential

Education involves a complex series of issues that tend to frame the enterprise. The major challenge is to figure out how to offer the best educational program for all the children while recognizing that an enterprise that is primarily financed through taxes cannot provide everything people might want.

A similar tension is felt by most people in regard to their personal finances and budgets. Most of us feel the challenge when we are forced to engage in a discussion of complicated and sometimes competing issues. This is particularly so when there are a variety of possible solutions and considerations, coupled with the need to be open minded yet thoughtful. In some settings philosophical debate may be the goal. When that is the case one can thoroughly enjoy the challenge and excitement of such a debate as an end in itself. When one is placed in an environment, such as a public school board setting where ultimately philosophical debate must come to a decision point, and in most cases fairly quickly, the decision can cause some consternation. This, particularly if the final decision is not the one most favored by a minority of the individuals participating in the debate.

7) Not a team player

One of the exciting reasons to be on the local school board is the opportunity to work with complex issues and challenges within a team environment. This can be a very exciting adventure for people who like this type of challenge. Issues that would fall into this category might include such things as:

- an effort to close a school – which school, when, why this school?
- discussion of reconfiguring schools to align grades with available space – why those grades, why now, is it necessary?
- efforts to control school spending – "not on our backs"
- employee grievances, arbitration and civil rights issues – union issues in general
- laying off or termination of employees
- patronage, nepotism pressures
- compliance audits – who made these rules anyway?
- handling public comments at Board meetings – personal, inappropriate, lengthy

- controversies regarding coaching decisions
  – "great coach, winning record should be taken
  into consideration"
- academic course content – sex education,
  creationism and evolution
- class size/teacher load – how many students
  are too many and in what subject areas is that
  number too many?
- environmental issues – trays in cafeteria, plastic
  utensils, placement of napkin dispensers.
- school security – policemen in school, are they
  needed, who pays, who supervises?
- inappropriate use of technology – whose
  standards apply?
- financial issues – balancing wants and needs
  with available resources
- what food will be served in the cafeteria?
- will carbonized drinks continue to be dispensed
  in school or will we move to fruit juices and
  milk?

There are volumes that could be written about most of these issues. How they are handled, who gets hurt by them, what are the final ramifications of the decisions that are made? These and other questions linger around each of these items. Most of them are complex and can be very challenging issues, yet in some sense fun to deal with particularly if they are handled by a group of people who are working as a team.
Several times it has been previously noted about the need for all board members to be committed to the separation of authority as it relates to policymaking by the Board of Education and the management of the district by the administrators. Failure to believe in, understand and work towards this separation of authority can prove disastrous.

Discussion of educational issues can be very enjoyable.

Discussion of educational issues can be very enjoyable. It can also be very stimulating. There should be value given to differing opinions and open resolution of conflict. Being on the minority end of a final board decision however can test the real strength and internal fortitude not only of the Board but sometimes the individuals involved.

8) Unable or unwilling to accept and support majority decisions.

Most boards prefer to work from a viewpoint that robust debate of the issues can be healthy. Most boards also prefer to work from the understanding that once a final vote is taken every board member will be supportive of the decision of the majority. If a person is not able to function in this manner, service on a board of education should probably not be given much thought. The inability or unwillingness of individual board members to support a majority decision has been the downfall of some significant board decisions and in some cases even a catastrophic problem for the school district. This really speaks to the question of teamwork and the ability of a person who is considering becoming a candidate for school board to become a member of the team.

Most people would like to think that when responsible caring adults have debated an educational issue and a majority decision is made board members would trust enough in their colleagues to support the decision. Unfortunately too many school districts can rehearse stories of "loose cannons" or "lone ranger" board members who would not or worse yet could not act in concert with their fellow board members. To some degree this unwillingness to accept the decision of the majority is viewed by these individuals as defeat. This is where the goal, to provide the best education possible for the children, is forgotten. Instead these people too often person-alize the "defeat" and wait for a "get even" occasion.

In one district the board had been discussing the reorga-nization of two of the districts elementary schools and the reassignment of an elementary principal for several meet-ings. The Superintendent had worked with the Administrators Association and the Building Principal involved and everyone was in agreement with the recommendation. When the Board finally approved the changes one board member who voted against the recommendation began a "crusade" to undermine the majority decision. Within a few days of the decision being made the board member and her husband, along with some friends filed an Appeal regarding the Board's decision before the Commissioner of Education in the State. When this happens the Board is obligated to answer the Appeal. As generally happens the local newspapers reported regu-larly on the "disagreement" among members of the Board of Education.

The Board took the opportunity as afforded under the Open Meetings Law to discuss various aspects of the district's defense of the Appeal in Executive Session. On more than one occasion the Board member who filed the Appeal was asked if she wanted to excuse herself from the Executive Session while the other Board members were discussing the Appeal. This Board member refused to avail herself of the opportunity afforded by the Board President to excuse herself from the discussion. Her action served to either seriously limit the discussion or let her know the next action planned by the Board attorney, as determined by the majority of the Board.

After several months and thousands of dollars in legal fees the Commissioner of Education dismissed the Appeal. In the next cycle of school board elections one of the friends of the referenced board member was elected to the Board. Another attempt was made to get the Board to reverse the earlier decision involving the realignment of the schools and the reassignment of one of the elementary principals. When this did not occur the two Board members filed another Appeal with the Commissioner of Education.

The next few months brought about a serious division among the board members themselves and some of the board members with the Superintendent. Again, after several months the Commissioner of Education denied the second Appeal. Unfortunately by this time irreparable harm had been done to board relationships, board and Superintendent relations and without doubt these ongoing activities had negatively impacted the educational process within the district.

These shenanigans also cost the taxpayers of the district tens of thousands of dollars. All because originally one board member was not willing to accept the decision of a majority of the board and wanted to press her opinion despite her minority position. This is a serious and costly example of a single board member's failure to accept and support the decision of the majority of the board.

9) Unwilling to be a progressive thinker

Another caution for someone who might consider becoming a school board candidate is this. If you are not a progressive thinker give up the idea now.

The famous last seven words of the church, "We've always done it that way before!" also apply to schools. If one is tied to the old ways, the one room school house model; "It was good enough for me" concept; industrial revolution models or "whatever money it takes, we will provide," don't even take out a petition to become a candidate for your local school board.

Anyone who is willing to take an unbiased look at the changes in our society over even the last twenty years will see that none of these models will suffice today.

More money is not the answer to every issue faced in education.

Don't assume that being a progressive thinker from my viewpoint means being willing to throw more money at every want or issue. If anything I believe boards, administrators and teachers unions in particular have been far too willing to see more money as the answer to nearly every issue faced in education. Simply put, "Money is not the answer to every issue faced in education."

In addition to progressive thinking we also don't have enough quality teachers, enough meaningful technology applications, or enough educational leaders to get the job done.

10) Having "Defeat" Difficulty

There was plenty written earlier about the ability a board member needs to accept defeat to one's stated position during a debate when the final vote is taken and the decision goes against your position. A candidate for school board also has to be able to deal with the fact that voters may not support their candidacy on voting day for whatever reasons. Voters' lack of support for one or more candidates leads to someone else being successful in the election. As stated much earlier, in as many as 50% of school district elections there are the same number of candidates as there are vacancies. If you choose to run in a district that has this circumstance then defeat in the election becomes impossible. For the good of the children and the voters of the district in terms of having a choice of board candidates one might conclude we are in fact advocating for situations that would increase the likelihood of there being defeats. In other words, more candidates running than vacancies available so naturally someone is going to be defeated. We are! The ability to deal with defeat thus becomes an issue to be reckoned with in more ways than one.

Before moving on let's take a look at some other issues that are not only important as a potential school board member but in fact make for an effective board of education.

Rational decision-making is the lifeblood of any school board. Boards have power and authority over a range of topics, and with this power goes the obligation to make the best decisions possible. It is no surprise that when board members are asked what makes them effective, they talk about the way they decide things, from virtually automatic appointments to potentially divisive issues.

An effective board of education also must function cohesively as a group. A healthy decision-making process naturally flows from board members working together to fulfill their responsibilities. When school board members gel as a unit they exhibit many characteristics of other well functioning groups: a shared respect and trust that recognizes the contribution of each individual, a feeling of cohesiveness, shared goals for the board, able leadership within the board often provided by the Board President, shared values and agreement on the board's operating rules.

In discussing their ability to act effectively board members will often speak of the need to negotiate the delicate balance between exercising authority and supporting the school districts chief executive, the Superintendent. Traditional governance wisdom suggests that you hire the best chief executive and then get out of his or her way. Sometimes the "…getting out of the way" becomes a real challenge. The superintendent's recommendation may be clearly contrary to the board's sense of what is important or supported by the community, or the superintendent may violate prior understandings of proposed action.

In one district the board and superintendent came to a complete stalemate on the proposed appointment of a building principal. Two final candidates were interviewed by the board and superintendent. The superintendent recommended one candidate. The board wanted to appoint the other candidate not recommended by the superintendent for this position. A stalemate ensued. Under State Law the superintendent could not make the appointment without board approval and the board could not make the appointment without the superintendent's recommendation.

At the end of the meeting neither side would move off its position despite a thoughtful, thorough discussion of the pros and cons of both candidates. As a result the meeting adjourned without a decision. By the next meeting an agreement had been reached that allowed an appointment to move forward. The superintendent agreed to recommend the candidate the board preferred to the particular building position and the board agreed to appoint the original choice of the superintendent to the next principal vacancy that occurred within the district. This agreement brought about a pleasant resolution to a situation that could have turned really ugly. In this case it showed the determination and willingness of the superintendent and the board to work together even though they initially disagreed on this important appointment.

An effective board also recognizes the importance of its role as a liaison between the district and the community. An effective board understands what the community wants and explains to the community what it believes to be in the best interest of all children.

Effective board members realize their important role as a liaison between the school district and the community.

The process works both ways. The long-established tradition of local control of education is based on the value of the community shaping its schools and of the schools belonging to the community. This close relationship hopefully contributes to greater community participation in the education of its children and an interest in how the schools operate.

As communities become more diverse so do their values. Building understanding and support becomes an increasing challenge. The board's role in explaining actions to the community and ensuring consideration of all points of view, while continuing to maintain the values, morals, ethics and viewpoint of the majority becomes increasingly important. I believe that failure to continue to include Judeo-Christian morals, values and ethics and the viewpoint of the majority in the public school system will ultimately lead us away from policies, procedures and programs that are in the best interests of the majority of people, particularly our children.

An effective board also is committed to working toward board improvement, which is self-improvement. This shouldn't be surprising. Forty percent of board members have three or fewer years of experience on the board. As a result they need to improve their performance as a board as the individuals gain more experience.

Finally board members need to act strategically. They need to discuss and resolve issues that are central to helping children learn. Planning systematically for the long term takes into consideration the needs and concerns of internal and external constituents all the while balancing reality in politics. Such a strategy matches plans against results and results against plans.

CHAPTER SEVEN

Step Up and Make a Difference

What is it going to take to make public education successful at least from the school board side of the equation? We believe it will take school board members who are forward thinking, frugal but not stingy, willing to let administrators administrate, willing to stand up to the teachers and other unions, willing to talk straight to politicians at all levels of government and willing to let parents be genuinely involved in the education of their children. Serving as a school board member is one of the most important responsibilities a citizen can undertake. Elected school board members have the opportunity to establish educational standards to shape the future of their community and society in general.

By this point there are probably questions about who can be a school board member. The qualifications are surprisingly simply. Anyone who is:

- A U.S. citizen
- At least 18 years of age
- Able to read and write
- A district resident for at least one year prior to the election
- Not employed by the board on which he serves.

But what are some of the personal characteristics a candidate for school board should possess? As mentioned previously rather than having a personal agenda or a "get even" attitude one should consider running for the school board to improve the quality of education. A potential candidate should recognize the importance of community service and exhibit a strong desire to "give back" to the community.

So what desirable qualities should a person considering running for the board of education have?

1) Desire to provide quality education for <u>all</u> children.

A good school board candidate needs first of all plain old common sense coupled with a sincere desire to give every child in the district a chance for a quality education. Board service gives the individual a real sense of purpose, even if for some it provides just a constructive use of leisure time.

School board members are required to take an oath to serve all the children of the state. In other words a quality education should not be reserved for only those children of parents who have special interests or those who make the most noise. Sometimes it is the quiet children and their parents who really need some advocacy. A good school board member needs to be an effective communicator and have the ability to be a consensus builder.

It is very helpful if a candidate has been an active community participant in some other organizations such as the local Parent Teacher Organization, the Athletic Boosters or a Shared Decision Making Team. Not only does such past experience help with name recognition in the election process but can also lend credibility to attempts to inform the general public about capital projects, budget issues and other sensitive items that require involvement and understanding from the community.

2) Committed to separation of authority

In the previous chapter reasons for not becoming a candidate for school board were discussed. One reason mentioned was knowing how to let administrators administrate. A significant quality of a good school board candidate is recognizing that as an individual board member they have no individual authority. As a board member they have one-fifth, one-seventh or one-ninth of the votes, depending on how many board members there are serving on the board.

Regardless of how knowledgeable a potential board member may be in their field, be it training, finance, business, the law or customer service for example, they probably don't know the school business. What's more as a school board member they really don't need to know "the school business."

The primary responsibility of a board member is to help the board set policy for the entire district and leave the management of the district to the professional administrators who are trained and certified in "school business."

There are far too many stories of board members who have crossed the line in this area. More than one School Business Official has told of a board member in his district, particularly one with a financial background, who felt the need to take data prepared by the Business Official and prepare their own financial charts and analysis of the same data for subsequent presentation to the Board.

Going even further, in some cases board members have publicly debated their analysis of the data versus the Business Officials data. One can imagine the impact of this behavior over a period of time, let alone the waste of time for everyone involved.

Another potentially tenuous situation is when a person who previously worked for a district becomes a board member. This phenomenon is occurring with more frequency. In this case the previous employee probably does know "the school business." Unfortunately sometimes they forget they have retired or moved to another place of employment. Here again, far too many stories abound of the outright danger of this circumstance.

In one large school district the previous Assistant Superintendent for Personnel became a board member shortly after he retired. He had a great deal of difficulty allowing his successor to change "his" processes and procedures. On more than one occasion the retired employee became a road-block to progress and refused to move past his own expe-riences. In this case his fellow board members, who had a great deal of respect for his previous service to the district, failed to have the courage to urge him to let the past be the past and move on. The Superintendent of the district also found himself in a difficult position. Here was a person who previously reported to him as an employee who was now in a position to evaluate him and determine his future salary and employment status. This made the probability of urging the former employee to leave these issues alone very difficult if not impossible for the Superintendent. Left unresolved the situation had a very detrimental effect on the district as well as the individuals involved. Ultimately the new Assistant Superintendent moved to another district.

In another school district the board told the Superintendent they wanted the new budget to increase no more than 3%. When the Superintendent began to cost out the known increases she quickly realized the 3% goal was absolutely impossible, The known increases included a 20% increase in employee health insurance, a 19% increase in Workers Compensation premiums plus previously negotiated contractual salary increases of 4% for the teachers in the district and 6% increase for all support staff. When she went back to the Board with these costs, specifically reminding them of the previously negotiated salary increases under the contracts which the Board of Education had approved, they retorted, "*This* Board did not approve those increases!" Factually that statement was correct because none of the currently serving board members were on the board when the contracts were approved. In reality however, the current board members representing the district had no choice but to honor the commitments of the previous board. This began an arduous struggle between the Board and the Superintendent which ended with an increased budget far beyond the 3% threshold and the resignation of the Superintendent. The proposed budget was also defeated initially. On a second vote carrying an approximate 17% increase, the budget was passed by district voters.

This whole situation brought about a very unsatisfactory and costly ending as a result of the hard, impractical stance of some very inexperienced board members.

3) A desire to help foster an environment that includes Judeo-Christian morals and ethics.

Many people in our society today who talk about the decline of public schools are quick to reference the lack of prayer in our schools. In their minds the answer to all the troubling issues currently facing our schools would be to simply re-institute the earlier patterns of prayer in school. Opponents of this position would cite the necessity and legal doctrine of the separation of church and state.

It's my opinion that this separation of church and state idea has been taken to an extreme which is really unnecessary. It actually has been used as a tool to drive religion from our schools. Having said that however I don't believe that simply reinstituting earlier patterns of prayer in school, even if legally possible, will solve all the issues of our schools. In a broader sense, I do believe that fostering an environment in our schools that includes Judeo-Christian morals and ethics will bring about a change in not only the behavior of students and adults in the school but in fact in our communities.

Simply reinstituting prayer in school will not solve all the issues of our schools.

After hearing a discussion of this idea on our weekly radio broadcast, one listener asked a great question via our website. The question was, "What are Judeo-Christian ethics?" The questioner wrote in part, "In hearing you talk about Judeo-Christian ethics I have many concerns. I am a practicing Christian but to me Judeo Christian family values is a code word related to specific values which are not agreed upon values across the Christian denominations. As a taxpayer I am not sure I would want values that I disagree with taught in a public supported school." The writer continued, "If I had children attending schools, I don't think I would want religious values I didn't agree with being taught to my children. Religious private schools are the schools where specific religious values should be taught."

Here is the response we gave to this listener. "Be assured that the words, Judeo Christian family values are not code words for anything on our part; they certainly are not intended to promote any particular religion or denomination. Our purpose is to encourage people that have core values such as honesty, truthfulness, selfishness, respect and caring to be involved in their local public school. We believe failure to include these values in the decisions that are made in schools and at the Board of Education level lead us away from what is in the best interest of the majority of people."

Currently there appears to be a high level of apathy or frustration among the general public towards our schools. As a result, viewpoints and beliefs that are held by a small minority of people, in some cases those who benefit directly from the decisions made and many times those who speak the loudest, have the strongest influence on the decisions that are made. In these circumstances the children of the district are often not benefited in any way. In fact, decisions that are made by some of these people may actually be detrimental to the children. This has proven true in the areas of curriculum, staffing, discipline, fairness to taxpayers and the overseeing of financial matters. Failure to have people involved in schools that have what some would call "old-fashioned" values at their core can lead to the erosion of basic principles and ultimately to anarchy.

As a result of these concerns I would suggest that another reason to become a school board member is to bring to the entire educational community a set of values, morals and ethics that are based on the Judeo Christian belief system.

4) A desire to work with others to increase academic standards

Unfortunately story after story can be related of school districts that have invited parents and other community members to a meeting when increasing academic standards has been announced as the topic. Very few if anyone accepted the invitation to the meeting. On the other hand let there be a controversy about the appointment of an athletic team coach or the possible cutting of an athletic team from the budget and the board room will be filled to capacity. What message does this type of response demonstrate about the importance of academics?

School districts need board of education members who will genuinely care about increasing academic standards and will hold district employees, particularly teachers and administrators, accountable for helping students achieve these increased academic standards. Although some frown on the business like term, this really has to do with the "return on investment" that the local tax payers receive. An important part of measuring achievement of these standards is constant reference to improving student test scores. Are the student's scores on local and state tests improving? A simple question but one that is seldom asked in some districts. The answer given to this simple question needs to be carefully analyzed by caring and knowledgeable board of education members. As a result of the No Child Left Behind federal legislation there has been a renewed interest in increasing academic standards and success for all students in meeting these more rigorous standards. Board service can fulfill this desire to work with others to increase academic standards and assist in helping all students meet these standards. In addition one also has the opportunity to work with other board members and the school administration to see that student test scores improve. This involves dealing with such controversial topics in some districts as "teaching to the test."

I have yet to figure out what teachers should teach to if not to the material that students will be tested on. However there remains much lively debate about this matter.

5) Balancing taxpayer affordability with financial needs.

There are several key words in this statement. Let's look at them individually. *Taxpayer Affordability.* Who decides what tax payers can afford? Can they afford more but are unwilling to pay? Do taxpayers have other priorities for their money and should they? These are difficult questions with no easy answer, at least not one that will satisfy everyone.

School districts receive its funds from primarily three sources, the Federal Government, State Government and local taxpayers. Do you notice any common thread among these three sources? Let me ask the question another way. Does the federal government have any money of its own? No, not unless you count the US mint where the government actually makes the money as federal money. Hardly a realistic claim. So the real answer to the question does the federal government have any money of its own is "No!" Does the state government have any money of its own? "No!"

Both the federal and state governments do have money which they collect through taxes. Both levels of government also spend some of this money on education. The source of most of the money is the taxpayers in our country or in our state. In other words, you and me. Who by the way are the same people who are considered the local taxpayers.

In recent years most school districts have received increased funds from the federal government, huge increases in state aid from the state, and yet have continued to ask local taxpayers to increase the amount of money they are paying for their schools.

It is difficult to arbitrarily say what the right amount of money is that the district should receive. It does seem to me however that in many cases school districts have hardly taken into consideration the major increases they have received from the federal and state government when they decided on the increases they are going to propose to the local taxpayer. The interesting part of this situation however is that district voters, in most districts have an opportunity to vote on the school budget and while they complain loudly about the increases they still vote for the budget. Frankly, to my dismay voters continue to support the increased budgets at a record pace.

School budgets will continue to be supported at this record pace if taxpayers fail to give school board members an indication, at least in a demonstrative way, that they are concerned about these increases and will not support them in the voting booth. As a result maybe it does fall on school board members to determine taxpayer affordability for the sake of those who elect them.

The other key words in the earlier statement are: *Financial Needs.* In a school setting how does one determine the difference between wants and needs? It may be easy to define basic building maintenance, reading supplies, textbooks and the like as needs in the school. It may not be

129

as easy to make the case to support financially staff development, public relations, elementary guidance or to answer such questions as: "At what grade level do we begin to teach foreign language? So, are these latter items wants or needs?

Frequently today when a conversation turns to the economy the ever increasing costs of financing schools inevitably crops up. Of particular concern are the increasing local property taxes. In school districts anywhere from 10% to 92% of the total costs of financing schools comes from the local property tax. The actual percentage is determined by the property and personal wealth of the local tax payers.

In many years when the inflation rate nationally hovered around 3% school increases in the local property tax more than doubled the inflation rate. The mind set of many people in education, particularly those who have responsibility for developing budgets seems to be that the ability of the taxpayer to pay the bill should not be a factor taken into consideration. The standard line is "The students of the district need these things for their education, so despite the costs, the taxpayers have an obligation to provide them." Teachers unions in particular are notorious for taking this position.

It seems to me the desire to balance taxpayer's affordability with financial needs of a school should be paramount. Unfortunately a school board candidate who thinks this way should be prepared for opposition from every union affiliated with the schools, most administrators and even fellow board members. The arguments can become sentimental, "Shouldn't we do all we can for the children" to down right demanding and personal. "You can't control costs on the backs of the teachers and others who have served the children of this district so faithfully for all these years."

These few paragraphs demonstrate clearly the difficulty of balancing taxpayer affordability with the financial needs of the school. This work however is part of the important tasks of a board member and needs to be done.

Is it possible that there may even be ways to improve education without a tax increase? Certainly Kenneth E. Hartman a board member in New Jersey thinks so. In a Commentary in the September 17, 2008 edition of <u>Education Week</u> Hartman offers the following suggestions, some I agree with others I strongly disagree with.

- **Control benefits and pension costs** – As salaries increase school staff members should be required to increase their contribution towards their health insurance. In districts where no contributions are currently made toward health insurance, contributions could be phased in and even prorated for new teachers who make less money than their senior colleagues. Pension benefits need to be reviewed as states are going deeper and deeper into debt to maintain a system that permits retirement at age 55, with a pension of up to 65 percent of the highest year's salary plus life time health-care coverage for the teacher retirees and often their spouses

I totally agree with this suggestion for the reasons Hartman offers.

- **Pay to Play** – Families should pay a small student-activity fee for their children to play a school sport, participate in a school club, or be in a school play. Families on free or reduced lunch program could be offered a fee waiver.

I totally disagree with this suggestion. If these activities are deemed necessary, appropriate and beneficial by the Board of Education as a part of the total education program all taxpayers should pay for them as part of the school budget.

- **Corporate and University Partnerships** – Hartman states, "State and Federal tax incentives are needed to entice corporations to financially support local schools. Colleges and universities could use their Federal Work-Study funds to pay their work-study students to serve as online tutors for local K-12 students, or offer online courses for schools to share."

I have a concern about offering anyone any more tax incentives given the current state of our economy. It has been my experience that colleges and universities already have plenty of opportunities on their campuses to utilize students on a Work-Study Program.

- **Create a K-11 graduation option** - Hartman maintains, "Millions of students are ready for college after completing 11th grade. Students who are ready for college could receive half the money a district would save by not educating them for another year in the form of a college scholarship."

The K-11 Option exists in some other countries like Canada and has worked very successfully. I would not support the notion of giving students half the money the district would save by not educating them. First of all this would have tremendous legal hurdles to get over plus if you are going to save the money, save it, don't give it away.

- **Stop reinventing the wheel** – An ever-changing curriculum is costly and has resulted in teachers being confused and suspicious of the "latest" new direction. The cost-benefit ratio of implementing a new curriculum every five to six years should be questioned by local school boards. Do we really need 15,000 curriculum departments?

I agree that curriculum does not need to be "ever-changing." It does need to be updated on a regular basis, particularly in certain areas like science and technology. I'm not sure where the 15,000 curriculum departments number comes from but I do agree that we could use less and still handle the curriculum needs of teachers.

- **Use the technology we bought** – Hartman states, "Nationally we have spent upwards of $60 billion on educational technology, with little evidence that it has had a significant impact on student achievement."

I agree that we have spent too much money on technology for the measureable return. We do need to use what we have to demonstrate the significant impact on student achievement. An example of this was in one district several years ago where the incoming Superintendent asked if every teacher in the district had a computer and an active email account. The answer was "Of course!" Upon further questioning it turned out there was a computer for each teacher in the district although most of them were still in their original shipping boxes stored in the school building. Every teacher did have an email address and internet access but no one could use the technology because the computer assigned to them had not been taken out of its box by the technology installers.

Hartman concludes his commentary by opining, "We can't afford not to operate a public school system that includes quality teachers, safe and functional facilities, and an internationally benchmarked curriculum. But, at the same time, we can't afford a system that we can't afford."

I agree!

Let me offer a final desirable quality people should have that are considering a run for their local school board.

6) Have the ability to make thoughtful, timely decisions.

Decisions simply have to be made. In some cases the decisions need to be made NOW! People who are indecisive or have difficulty bringing themselves to a decision point are generally not good board of education members.

Some would go so far as to call people who have difficulty making a decision "procrastinators or blockers." That may be a bit harsh but non-decision makers do inhibit progress and in some cases actually become a stumbling block.

Many people have worked on committees and in other group settings where there is someone who always "... needs more information." This also happens on boards of education. While not suggesting that board members should not be thoughtful and deliberate in their decision making, I am convinced there are some board members who are afraid, unable or unwilling to make a decision, particularly a timely one on almost anything. As a result they slow all decisions down to a snails pace because they "...need more information" or need to "mull the situation over until the next meeting." While in themselves these are not bad things, if used to excess or with the purpose of stalling a decision they are probably not good things. Such behavior is not only unproductive but can in fact be hurtful. In some cases contract deadlines and grant application deadlines have been missed. Failure to make a decision in situations like these can result in the loss of thousands of dollars. Such behavior should be called out by others who see it, particularly fellow board members.

Someone who is considering becoming a school board member needs to know themselves well enough to know if they have the ability to make thoughtful, timely decisions. Having this ability can contribute a great deal towards being a productive board member.

Boards are sometimes confronted with difficult and even controversial decisions that can generate a lot of emotion. People who know that generally also know that nothing worthwhile comes easy and will end up enjoying the contribution they can make to their school and their community.

In an article entitled "The Servant Leader" published in the October 2008 edition of American School Board Journal, authors John Cassel and Tim Holt cite the most significant characteristics of a servant leader. People considering running for their local school board would do well to consider whether they have these important characteristics.

a) **Listening** – School board members sit between the community and the district, facilitating communication between the two. The board tells a community story to the district and the district story to the community. Many experienced board members have learned that too much speaking and not enough listening will not get the job done. Deep, careful listening ensures all voices are heard and encourages true dialogue about critical issues.

b) **Healing** - schools have a remarkable record of connecting to some of society's toughest problems, race, poverty, immigration, and changes in the American family. Many people have been hurt by schools. It is not surprising there is a need for healing. A healthy district truly serves students, staff, and community and confront some of the tough issues that have created collateral damage.

c) **Persuasion** - school boards have tremendous power, but successful boards exercise their power as persuasion rather than coercion.

d) **Foresight** - a key role of the board is to focus on the future. The board uses the horizon to keep the district on course and refuses to allow day-to-day concerns to pull attention away from the horizon. It is often hard to see the future implications of today's decisions and trends but the board's exercise of servant leadership is the best viewpoint available.

e) **Commitment to people** - schools like most institutions are about the people who staff them. Teachers who know instruction and focus on learning; principals who care about a well articulated curriculum, student achievement and staff development; other administrators who care about the district culture and serving the students and community; support staff who understand how important their roles are — all are key to a high performing district. "Servant leader" boards are like orchestra conductors who know they don't make the music, they lead the musicians in making it. "Servant leader" boards focus on strengthening the capacity of the people in the institution, the capacity to learn, teach, to contribute.

f) **Community building** - the oft stated African proverb has it right: "It takes a village." So, whether you start from the student side and work to draw in community resources, or from the community side where you quickly realize the centrality of good schools, the more connected and strong the community and schools, the better. Servant leader board members work within the district to build the foundation of good communication, good relationships, and clarity about roles.

Here are some final thoughts that should be considered by anyone thinking about becoming a candidate for their local school board. A candidate should feel strongly that every child can achieve and ask at all times, as a former mentor of mine always did "is it good for kids?" A candidate should have a primary motivation to serve on the board for the purpose of maintaining and improving the educational system for all children.

Additionally one needs to be able to recognize and respect the individual strengths and differences of each board member and support everyone's right to freely express opinions. This doesn't mean, nor should it, that all board members will always agree on everything. It should mean however that there can be disagreements on issues but there will be a commitment to always maintain respect and trust for other board members and the Superintendent.

Board candidates also need to understand not only the need, but the legal requirement of confidentiality on issues such as personnel, pending litigation and contracts, that can be discussed only during closed Executive Sessions of the board. Failure to maintain this confidentiality can be extremely damaging not only to the district but to the individuals involved as well.

Recently a school board member in a very large City School District leaked alleged conversation that had occurred during an Executive Session related to the reasons for dismissal of a coach. Once the conversation was leaked some other board members took it on themselves to state, "That conversation never took place during the Executive Session in question." One can imagine the reaction of the former coach and the public to this situation. The dismissed coach has now hired an attorney and no doubt will be filing a lawsuit. The illegal action of this board member has now forced the district to spend money to defend itself in the pending lawsuit.

Education Law does give the Board of Education authority to bring charges against a fellow board member for such action however this action is very seldom taken. In this particular case a private investigator has been hired to determine the source of the "leak." The taxpayers will pay all the costs for this investigation. All this expense brought about as a result of one board member acting inappropriately and perhaps illegally.

A school board candidate should also be prepared to contribute to having board meetings operate in a dignified, professional manner in which everyone is treated with civility and respect. Name calling, foul language and the like have no place at a school board meeting. Among a variety of reasons these behaviors should not occur is the negative example being set for students who are often in attendance at the meetings. In the same vein board members need to be able to interact with other board members and the Superintendent in a positive, constructive, helpful manner. As mentioned earlier, in New York State nearly a quarter of the sitting Superintendents indicate this type of obnoxious behavior occurs in their district with some regularity. Several years ago in one district a physical fight, including the exchange of punches by board of education members took place.

In an effort to bring stability to a district a candidate should also be willing to serve at least two terms in office if at all possible. Most sitting board members will say that it took them at least two years to feel totally comfortable in their new role. Obviously lots of things happen in school. The interesting part of serving as a board member is that many things happen only once a year. In other words most things that happen during the first year are new to a board member. School begins once a year, budgets are built once a year, new board members join the board once a year, leadership of the board changes once a year, statewide school report cards are received once a year, an annual audit is performed and reported once a year. As a result, to gain experience in these matters, a new board member is at least into their second year of their term before they experience these things are repeated.

Given all the requirements, characteristics and personality traits that seem to be part of the desirable makeup of a person considering becoming a candidate for school board, it would be fair to ask if there is any return on investment for the candidate? Obviously any return would be in a nonmonetary manner.

Below is a list of possible returns on their investment as a school board member. An article in the <u>American School Board Journal</u> April 2008 written by Doug Eadie and entitled "The Board Member's ROI" form the basis for this list.

1) The first return on investment (ROI) for a board member can be the satisfaction that comes from playing a meaningful role in doing high impact governing work that makes a significant difference in the districts affairs, especially in terms of student achievement.

2) Board members also have the right to expect to grow in terms of their leadership capacity through their school board service. They should expect to acquire knowledge and skills that will make them a more effective participant in their community or perhaps at the state and national levels.

3) Most board members experienced significant satisfaction. Many people that run for school boards have significant ego needs. One can expect to be publicly recognized in your role as a top leader of your district, front and center at the ribbon-cutting ceremonies for the new school, quoted in the newspaper series on the contribution of education in your communities economically development efforts or perhaps even interviewed on a morning talk show. Public speaking can be an immensely ego satisfying experience for board members provided that they are adequately supported in their work at the podium.

4) Hopefully board members will also experience some fun along with the hard work required as part of their

service. The Superintendent can help by making sure that you are kept abreast of exciting developments at the national and state level in K-12 education. A more serious commitment to enriching the governing experience is for your board to budget for members to attend state and national conferences. Such experiences should be reviewed as working experiences however and not as a playtime at taxpayer expense.

One of the important and difficult aspects of the work of the Teaching and Learning Institute is to find ways to identify people who have the necessary characteristics and attributes to become a school board candidate.

There is a lot more to say about finding qualified people to run for school board. Our thoughts on this important topic begin in the next chapter.

CHAPTER EIGHT

School Board Candidates – Where Are They?

The research done by the Teaching and Learning Institute has shown that a very important way to get people to consider a run for school board is to have a sitting school board member approach them about it. As a result we believe that candidates who are successful in their campaign and gain a seat on the board should place a high priority on encouraging other outstanding citizens to run for the school board.

The American School Board Journal, March 2004 in an article entitled "Finding the Best" authored by Cronin, Goodman and Zimmerman, suggested the following professional characteristics for people considering a run for school board.

1) Understand the board's proper role and resists attempts to micromanage.
2) Be prepared to serve as liaison between the school system and community.
3) Shield the superintendent from undue political pressure.
4) Help ensure that board meetings and other board work focus on improving student achievement.

5) Support the board's key role in policy making, developing a vision and goals, community engagement, budget adoption, and fiscal responsibility.
6) Understand that individual board members have no authority unless delegated by the board. Under state law, only a quorum of the board has authority to act and to make decisions at an officially called board meeting.

The New York State School Board Association offers these answers to the question, "What makes a good school board member?"

- **Effective communicator** - can describe what he or she wants and describe what others want; a good listener
- **Consensus builder** - capable of working towards decisions that all can support and willing to compromise to achieve that goal.
- **Community participant** - enjoys meeting a variety of people, can identify the communities key communicators and reaches out to the community.
- **Decision maker** - knows his or her own as well as others decision-making styles, can support group decision-making
- **Information Processor** - can organize priorities and schedules to handle lots of verbal and written information
- **Leader** - willing to take risks, be supportive of board colleagues, district staff and community.
- **Team player** - helps promote the board's vision and goals.

So where do school districts find such people, or is it even the districts responsibility to look for these people? Whose responsibility is it? How are potential candidates identified and cultivated?

Answers to these questions are challenging. I believe that's part of the reason why as many as 50% of board vacancies have only one candidate vying for election.

As an Adjunct Faculty member at the State University of New York (SUNY) at Brockport in the Educational Administration Program, answering these questions has proven to be a challenging assignment for graduate students. I have had the privilege of teaching these students who are completing their administrative certification requirements. Here are some of their thoughts on the question, "Where do school districts find good school board candidates?

One graduate student and current Special Education Administrator in a small city school district wrote. "Being a board member is not the same today as it was in the early 1900's. The earliest school boards were designed with one purpose and that was to find and hire teachers. Now, board members are asked to serve the community on committees for buildings and grounds, budget and finance, policy, technology, personnel, negotiations and so much more. There are more state and federal regulations, a much more diverse student and community population, students with more complex needs and much higher expectations from the community that the public schools should do more for their children, often with less money. This is also an unpaid position. The responsibilities and pressures of serving on today's school board have probably contributed to the low number of candidates interested in running for the school board."

Another grad student went on to say, "Ultimately, the school board, superintendent, administrators and even teachers need to reach out to the community to spark an interest. By advertising in the local newspaper, on the radio and even local television, many more people will be aware that there is an interest in the community to acquire more

Board candidates. The minimal qualifications should be mentioned, even highlighted, so that the majority of the community will understand that they could be potential candidates.

When using the local paper, radio or television advertisers should be sure to include children. When a child's voice is heard on the radio it's difficult to ignore. Similarly, an advertisement with children asking community members to volunteer would be inviting. Currently, candidate qualifications, board responsibilities and the fact that vacancies exist are not widely published. By utilizing a variety of media schools can get this information out to the community. Similarly, local businesses and organizations can post or pass out flyers with the appropriate information.

Perhaps the most productive way to recruit board candidates is through good public relations. Current board members, superintendents, the administrative team, teachers and support staff should be active in spreading the word about the need for more Board candidates. All of the above mentioned have their own social circles and while they are discussing the position and the qualifications districts will have a well-informed community and perhaps more candidates."

Other ideas suggested by this student include this one. "Most schools hold an open house in which they invite the parents and even other community members into the school buildings. This would be a great time to present information to the community about the Board of Education. Current board members and even a few students could share information about the board and instructions on how to run for a seat on the board. Another option might be to hold a "Meet the Board" night.

Scandalous and negative news may be what sells papers but it can cripple the school district.

No matter how much energy and effort is put into recruiting new Board candidates, people just will not consider running if the board is painted in a bad light in the area. The local newspaper can make or break the board's image. Scandalous and negative news may be what sells papers but it can also cripple the school district. The effects of focusing on and reporting mostly negative news on school boards and superintendents are far-reaching. Such reporting can certainly negatively impact people's thoughts about considering the idea of becoming a candidate for the school board."

Another student and Athletic Director in a district in the Southern Tier of New York State opined, "The single most important factor to consider when developing a strategy for increasing the number of candidates for the Board of Education is building relationships. Building relationships both inside and outside of the school allows school leaders to more effectively advocate for education and young people. So the mission of increasing the number of candidates for the Board of Education begins with building relationships. It is the first critical step toward building a strong school district and promoting a strong community."

This student went on to suggest that to accomplish the mission stated above, three key factors need to be addressed:

1) increasing community support and active involvement in the district
2) promoting and educating the community on the importance and satisfaction experienced from board service

145

3) cultivating a collaborative healthy climate among existing board members.

The first step in increasing the number of candidates for the Board of Education is to increase community support and involvement in the school district. The district needs to develop and implement a plan for increasing this support and involvement in its schools. A great way to do this is through encouraging volunteerism.

Volunteerism in school declines as potential volunteers' children progress into middle and high school.

Unfortunately, volunteering in general often declines as potential volunteers' children progress into middle and high school. The school district needs to develop a plan to address this decline and help keep parents involved throughout their child's school years.

School district personnel can begin by identifying potential board of education candidates from the volunteer pool. People should then work to groom them for future service in the district, by recognizing these volunteers' accomplishments. It is also helpful to get their names out in the public so others know who they are when election time comes.

At the same time the Board of Education is building relationships and gaining community support and community involvement the district should be introducing and educating the community on the benefits and satisfaction of Board of Education service.

It is important for the district to be proactive in publicizing the process necessary to become a candidate for the Board of Education. Contacting local media sources to run advertisements concerning the process including petitions, timelines and expenditure reporting can help to foster better understanding and can help potential candidates become more comfortable with these activities.

It is also very important to start speaking with potential candidates early in the school year to determine their readiness and willingness to run. Through this ongoing development process the school district is continually identifying and preparing candidates.

Another graduate student, the Dean of Students in a large suburban district took a very different approach to the recruitment of potential board of education members. The student decided to research what sitting school superintendents thought about involving themselves in the process.

The student emailed a survey to all sitting school superintendents in one county in the Southern Tier of New York State. He had a very healthy 59% response rate to the survey. Fifty seven percent of the districts reported that it had a hard time finding quality candidates to run for the school board in their community. Forty three percent of schools reported that over the past five elections, they only had one race for a board seat. Another 43% of the other schools reported that twice over the last five years they had a race for only one seat.

All of this limited specific research verifies the research results obtained by the Teaching and Learning Institute in its study of school districts on a much broader scale.

Superintendents should not be involved in the recruitment of potential school board members.

Another question on the survey asked if the superintendent should have any involvement in recruiting candidates to run for the school board. All the superintendents responding said "No!" They all thought it was the responsibility of current school board members to do the recruiting.

Two superintendents when pressed did offer a strategy to help increase board candidates within their school. One superintendent stated, "My strategy would be to ask residents in casual conversation if they would be willing to serve on the board of education. If they indicated any interest whatsoever I would tell that individual what characteristics would be an asset for a person working on the board. I would then pass the names of those individuals indicating even a slight interest on to a current board member so one or more of the current members could discuss this opportunity with them."

The other superintendent stated, "I would put pressure on current board members to recruit people. Advertise as much as possible. Put notices in the district newsletter, and suggest to staff that they might be on the look-out for community members who might make a good board member and then encourage them to talk to these people about becoming a candidate."

This same graduate student came to some intriguing conclusions as a result of his research. He concluded, "Superintendents' involvement when it comes to recruiting perspective board members is something that is very delicate in the eyes of some superintendents and badly needed in the eyes of others. This issue is at times a dilemma every school leader faces because the superintendent's future depends on the direction new school board members will want to take and their relationship with him.

As superintendents go longer into their time in the school district there is more chance for turnover on the board. Research shows that during the third and fourth year of a superintendent's tenure, as many as 1/3 to 1/2 of the school board members who originally selected the superintendent do not seek reelection to the Board. This change in the make up of the Board of Education may be a significant change over or it may be more subtle. Often a new dynamic or chemistry occurs which can have a direct impact on the possibility of the superintendent continuing to serve in that district."

In another study conducted by Jack McKay and Horace Mann at the University of Nebraska, the researchers found that half of the surveyed superintendents reported they would communicate indirectly to other school board members about securing potential board candidates rather than go out into the communities themselves. At the same time, the other half of the superintendents thought it was not necessary to be involved in the process at all with one stating, "Superintendents should not be involved in the selection or election process. I've known some that did and they didn't remain in their jobs long. It is political suicide to be involved in this process." Another superintendent stated, "I believe that smart superintendents try to manage the process through other board members but do not become directly involved in recruiting themselves."

As you can see there are very differing views about where school board candidates can be found and how they can be nurtured once they are found. The important thing is if you or someone you know is interested in the possibility of becoming a school board candidate you need to read the next chapter.

CHAPTER NINE

So What Is the Next Step?

My hope is that after reading this far you are to the point of wanting to know more about becoming a school board candidate. If you are, I am thrilled. Obviously there is a lot to know. Let's begin with some basics.

It is important to know the timelines for developing your candidacy and filing the required papers. These timelines will vary from state to state. The first timeline mentioned here would be typical for school board elections in New York State but are probably similar in other states. The second timeline cited is for school board elections in Pennsylvania.

New York State Model

During the time period from January to March a person who is considering a run for the local school board should begin attending some Board of Education meetings if this has not been done previously. This would help them gather information about the issues the board is currently dealing with and the makeup and dynamics of the board. During this same time it's possible to find out which current Board members terms are expiring and perhaps even if the incumbents are planning to run for another term. This is obviously important information because as is true in most elected positions incumbents have a distinct advantage.

During the period from February to April potential candidates should be circulating petitions for signatures by residents of the district. The number of signatures required and the actual date for the submission of the petitions can be secured from the District Clerk of the school district. We recommend securing more than the minimum required signatures in case there is a problem with any of the signatures submitted. A challenge to a signature or signatures on the petition that is upheld could result in the potential candidate not having the required minimum signatures on the approved petition which would result in the candidate being disqualified from running in the election.

School Board Election Day and the vote on school budgets is always the third Tuesday in May.

As mentioned previously all school districts in New York State have 5, 7 or 9 board members. Terms of office are either three or five years and are generally staggered to provide for continuity of service of board members.

Pennsylvania State Model

In Pennsylvania the process and timeline for becoming a school board candidate, also called "directors" is quite different. All school boards in Pennsylvania have nine members who each serve a four year term. The election process calls for five members being eligible for election or re-election during one election cycle and four being eligible in the next cycle. This 5-4 rotation prevents having nine new members on a school board and ensures continuity on the board.

School districts may elect board members in three ways: at large, by region or by a combination of these. If board members are elected at large, they may live anywhere in the district and be elected for any position. If a region plan is approved, school directors who reside in the region are elected by and from each region. Where a combination at large and region plan is approved all regions have an equal number of school directors who reside in each region and elected by each region.

To become a school board candidate, one must file a petition signed by at least 10 qualified voters of the school district for the political party with which the petition will be filed.

Primary elections usually are held on the third Tuesday in May. In Presidential election years, the primary is held in April. School board elections occur in November of odd-numbered years.

More detailed information on running for school board in Pennsylvania can be obtained at www.psba.org

As you can read the differences between New York State and Pennsylvania are significant. Of particular significant difference is the involvement of political parties in Pennsylvania.

In preparation for the election in any state a candidate should prepare a well written well thought out paper on their reasons for their interest in serving on the board and why they would make a good board member.

The candidate should also develop a strategy for promoting her campaign. This may include preparing for an appearance on Candidates Night if the district holds one. It may also involve printing and distributing fliers, posters and mailings.

To get elected a candidate needs to be talking to people about their candidacy. Here are some questions a potential candidate for their local school board might ask themselves.

1. What is it in my background and/or personal experience that would enable me to contribute to the working of the school board as a whole?

153

2. What do I consider to be a significant contribution that I have already made to our community that I would like others to know about?
3. What other information regarding my experience, qualifications and contribution would I like others to know?

The Teaching and Learning Institute is committed to helping people who have any level of interest in possibly becoming a candidate for their local school board. We are particularly interested in those people who would bring Judeo-Christian ethics and values to their candidacy.

The Chapter 11 of this book specifically outlines the Strategic Plan and Mission of the Teaching and Learning Institute. Before we get to that let's talk about What's So Great About Public Education?

CHAPTER TEN

What's So Great About Public Education?

A fter all the words about public education and encouraging people to get more involved it seems fitting to include some answers to the question, What's So Great About Public Education? It is necessary to answer this question because so many people today can't seem to find many good things to say about public education. Perhaps it's more accurate to say most people can only find negative things to say about it.

In an effort to make the case for public education and to hopefully solidify your interest, perhaps even your commitment to become more involved, here are just a few things that are great about public education.

1. **Well developed academic program.**

   a) A testing program requirement at most grade levels that compares learning and student achievement to students in similar grades both statewide and nationwide.

b) Rigorous exit examinations that assure that graduates can enter college or the world of work with the academic preparation they need.

c) An increasing number of school districts high school students can graduate with numerous college credits earned through either the Advanced Placement Program or area college credit earned via distance learning. In some cases students have graduated with enough college credits to have them enter a quality four year institution as a second semester sophomore. Not only does this give the student a tremendous advantage but it has the potential to save the students and their parents upward of $50,000.

d) Most schools now require some form of community service as criteria for graduation. Such a requirement gives high school students the opportunity to be involved in their community in a meaningful way. Volunteerism in general is declining in most communities. By requiring high school students to volunteer they will have practical experience which may encourage them to continue to provide community service or volunteer long after they graduate from high school.

2. Sophisticated level of technology

a) Almost every public school is required to have an Acceptable Use Policy which must be signed and adhered to by all student, faculty, staff and even Board of Education members who have access to or utilize the districts' computer network.

b) The district network contains high levels of safeguards, filters, blockers and monitoring systems and software.

c) Basic computer skills are taught by a qualified teacher at an early age. More advanced computer skills are taught at age appropriate levels.

d) Various types of technology hardware (computers, IPods, cell phones) are integrated into the instructional and learning process by many teachers.

e) A wide variety of software is utilized by both teachers and students.

f) Student assignments are often required to be completed using technology applications.

g) Lots of parent to teacher communication occurs via the Internet and email. (Homework assignments, project lists etc.)

3. A plethora of music, athletic and social opportunities are available

a) A high level of music instruction is available to all students who are interested. Small group lessons as well as large ensembles in band, orchestra and chorus, conducted by certified music teachers comprise the musical opportunities. The most talented and gifted musicians have the opportunity to participate in State and National ensembles.

b) Most districts fund multiple sports teams with age and school size appropriate competition. These teams provide students with the opportunity to learn team work and the meaning of fair competition.

c) School sponsored clubs and organizations such as the National Honor Society, Future Farmers of America, Students Against Drunk Driving and the Vocational Industrial Clubs of America give students an opportunity to learn leadership skills along with academic development in a competitive environment.

4) Increasing student expectations

a) Over the last few years most public school districts have drastically increased the requirements for graduation. These increases include not only the total number of course credits required but increased course requirements in the areas of math and science.

b) All schools in the nation are being monitored and held accountable by the Federal Government for student achievement, graduation requirements and the rigor of classroom instruction.

c) A requirement for additional and meaningful student homework has been added in many school districts.

5) Dedicated, caring professional teachers and staff members

Perhaps as with any organization the people in the public school systems of America really make the difference. During my many years of involvement in the public school system beginning as a student, then parent, teacher and administrator I have enjoyed working with some of the finest people to be found anywhere in the world. I have seen people go far beyond anything that could be reasonably expected or asked of an employee in an effort to serve the students, parents and community members at large. I have seen "people of faith" act out the commands of Christ to be "salt and light" as well as "bearers of the truth." This is a good thing!

Chapter Eleven

What is the Teaching and Learning Institute?

In 2005, after several months of prayer and dreaming, the Teaching and Learning Institute, legally known as TLI Inc., was born. As mentioned earlier in Chapter One, TLI was created by public school administrators who collectively had nearly 50 years experience in the public school systems of New York State. We have served the children of the state in school districts ranging from small to large in rural, suburban and small city locations.

We have seen moral and ethical standards decline.

During our careers we have also seen drastic changes in public education. Some changes have been less than desirable, other changes have certainly been for the good of all involved. Here are some examples of some of the changes we have seen.

We have seen state mandates and expectations for students increase dramatically and fortunately have seen students respond positively.

We have seen the costs of education skyrocket.

We have seen communities demand more and more of school districts and their personnel.

We have also seen less and less involvement and responsibility taken by parents.

We have seen moral and ethical standards decline.

We have seen more and more school boards lose sight of the reason they were created.

We have seen more and more school board members struggle to take over responsibilities which are not theirs to take.

TLI Inc. was created to help address many of these areas. Our mission statement and strategic plan outline our purposes and goals as well as the methods we are currently using to achieve them.

The Mission of the Teaching and Learning Institute is:

1) To increase the number of candidates who are willing to run for their local school board.

2) To identify teaching candidates who will champion high ethical standards and promote these standards throughout the entire employment process.

Candidates whether for the Board of Education or for teaching should be committed to family values based on a traditional Judeo-Christian belief system.

The Strategic Plan of the Teaching and Learning Institute is to:

- Develop awareness of the need for increased numbers of school board candidates who are committed to family values based on a traditional Judeo-Christian belief system.
- Provide regular television, radio and newspaper advertisements publicizing the opportunities available to people who are interested in becoming a candidate for their local school board or teacher candidates in the public school system.
- Make written opinion pieces related to current educational issues available to newspapers on a periodic basis.
- Offer a variety of presentations to community groups interested in learning more about supporting traditional family values in our public schools.
- Offer training sessions to individuals who may be considering running for their local Board of Education.
- Encourage political leaders at the federal, state and local levels to support legislation that encourages family values based on a traditional Judeo-Christian belief system.
- Monitor proposed legislation in the New York and Pennsylvania State Legislature dealing with character education, moral issues, religion and ethics as it relates to PreK-12 education in the State and offer advice and counsel on these matters.
- Identify teaching candidates who will champion high ethical standards and promote these standards throughout the entire employment process.

- Conduct training sessions on writing a great resume and cover letter for individuals who may be considering a teaching career.
- Offer resume critique services and support to teacher candidates.

One of our major efforts to expand our influence and effort has been through the opportunity extended by the Family Life Radio Network (FLN) headquartered in Bath, NY. On the network we offer a Christian perspective on a wide variety of current public education issues in a weekly interview/discussion format. TLI is also frequently requested to offer commentary on various current issues in education that are mentioned on the news broadcasts on FLN. The Family Life Radio Network currently owns 14 stations and 52 translators. It engages a regular listening audience of 250,000 and has a potential audience to reach 4 million people daily throughout New York State and Pennsylvania.

As a direct result of this radio opportunity in 2007 we expanded our initial efforts in New York State into Pennsylvania with its 501 school districts. From our conversations with Pennsylvania residents it appears that most of the issues of concern in New York State are also of concern in Pennsylvania.

In subsequent conversations with people from various parts of the country and from our research we have concluded that many of the issues initially recognized in New York State are the same educational issues and concerns throughout our country.

The Teaching and Learning Institute continues to look for practical ways to implement our Strategic Plan. This book is part of that expanded effort. It was written with a very specific intention. That intention was to address the multitude of issues currently being faced by the public schools of our nation. Hopefully the book will be helpful in offering practical steps for parents, students, educators and also government and community leaders to make a positive impact on their local public schools.

The authors' desire is that **The Sin of Apathy** will also serve as an ongoing challenge of the need for citizen involvement in their local public school, particularly by people who are committed to family values based on a traditional Judeo-Christian belief system.

If you have been challenged in this way by these words I am eternally grateful and feel my work has been successful.

We are anxious to receive your comments, feedback and reaction to this book. We are also anxious to help you or other interested people to sort through the process of becoming a school board candidate.

For these or any other reasons we welcome your communication. The Teaching and Learning Institute (TLI Inc.) can be contacted in a variety of ways.

Website: www. teachingandlearninginstitute.org
Email: tli@frontiernet.net
Telephone: 585-567-2080
Mailing Address: P.O. Box 32, Houghton, NY 14744

TLI Inc. is a privately funded organization not affiliated with any other existing organization. We never ask for financial assistance from anyone who contacts us. All of our resources and materials are available at no cost to the recipients.

Printed in the United States
210780BV00001B/1/P